BAE

Untold Night and Day

TRANSLATED FROM THE KOREAN BY
Deborah Smith

VINTAGE

1 3 5 7 9 10 8 6 4 2

Vintage is part of the Penguin Random House group of companies whose addresses can be found at global.penguinrandomhouse.com

First published in Korea as 알려지지 않은 밤과 하루 by Jaemgua Mouem in 2013

First published in Vintage in 2021
First published in the UK by Jonathan Cape in 2020

penguin.co.uk/vintage

A CIP catalogue record for this book is available from the British Library

ISBN 9781529110869

This book is published with the support of the Literature Translation Institute of Korea (LTI Korea)

Printed and bound in Great Britain by Clays Ltd, Elcograf S.p.A.

The authorised representative in the EEA is Penguin Random House Ireland, Morrison Chambers, 32 Nassau Street, Dublin D02 YH68.

Penguin Random House is committed to a sustainable future for our business, our readers and our planet. This book is made from Forest Stewardship Council® certified paper.

MIX
Paper from responsible sources
FSC
www.fsc.org
FSC® C018179

I

The former actress Ayami was sitting on the second flight of stairs in the audio theatre, with the guestbook in her hand.

She was alone. At that point, nothing else had been made known.

With the lights off, the interior of the auditorium seemed as though submerged in murky water. Objects, matter itself, were softly disintegrating. All identity became ambiguous, semi-opaque. Not only light and form, but sound, too. The auditorium held only five two-seater sofas; other than that, the irregular flights of stairs served as a public gallery.

Sitting in this same spot with the guestbook open in front of her, after the day's performance was over and she had closed the theatre doors; this time was precious to Ayami. Not that the audience members usually wrote down anything special. Now and then, a blind visitor might record something using Braille, but Ayami could not decipher such language. Still, she didn't sit with the book in her hand in order to read but to listen, quietly, to a voice that faded in and out.

> Don't go far away, even for just one day, because
> Because . . . a day is long, and
> I will wait for you.[*]

Ayami was sitting alone in the auditorium because always, at this time of day, an old radio hidden somewhere among the sound equipment turned itself on. Since Ayami was afraid of the static electricity that sparks in machines, cables, microphones and speakers, and believed the disturbance caused by sound waves was able to inflict physical damage, she couldn't conceive of touching or even peering at the backs of the bulky machines to look for a radio, deliberately concealed among them or just left there by mistake. Though she worked at the audio theatre, her familiarity with the sound equipment only extended to putting the CD of a given performance into the stereo and pressing 'play'. Now and then, a sound engineer from the foundation would come to check that everything was in working order, but Ayami had never spoken with him.

The engineer wore a baseball cap jammed right down on his head, obscuring his face and making him look like a shadow of himself. He always came on the shuttle bus, even though he never brought any heavy equipment, and there was never anyone else with him. The bus was white, and emblazoned with the foundation's logo. The theatre

[*] Pablo Neruda, *100 Love Sonnets*, Sonnet 45, partly modified

director was informed in advance of the precise time of the engineer's visit, so that any issues could be discussed in person. The director came out to greet the engineer when he arrived, and saw the bus off when he left.

One time, Ayami had wanted to tell the director about the radio, how it switched itself on and off again. It hadn't yet happened during a performance, but there would be a problem if it did, and Ayami felt the director ought to be informed, given that he was her only colleague and superior.

Pausing outside the open door to the director's office, as though the thought had only just occurred to her, Ayami turned and said, 'There's probably some kind of issue with one of the wires. Maybe a cable for the speakers got connected to this radio by mistake.'

The director looked up from his desk.

'There's no radio there that I know of. And it's strange; I've never heard this sound you're talking about. Then again, I can't claim to be blessed with especially acute hearing.'

'Well, I'm not completely sure it's coming from a radio.' Ayami wavered, but she'd started now and felt compelled to carry on. 'I'm just guessing. In any case, now and then, when the theatre's very quiet, you can hear something – well, no, I suppose all I can say for a fact is that it feels like you can hear something.'

'What are we talking about, specifically? Music?'

'No, not that. It sounds like someone reading a book out loud, very slowly; like distant muttering, yes, like someone talking to themselves . . . a monotonous voice, like the one that reads the shipping forecast, purposefully speaking slowly so that the fishermen have time to make a note of the predictions. South-easterly waves 2.5 metres, south-westerly, slight cloud, rainbow to the south, rain shower, hail, north-easterly, 2, 35, 7, 81 . . . at least, that's how it seems to me.'

'And you usually hear this sound in the evenings, after the performance is over and the sound equipment's been switched off?'

'Yes.'

'In that case, mightn't it be a sound shadow, left behind after the performance?'

'A sound shadow?'

'Like an unknown voice.'

Ayami stared hard at the director, but couldn't tell whether he was joking or being sincere. Thinking how little she knew about machines, she was still wondering how she ought to respond when he saved her the trouble.

'When the engineer comes the day after tomorrow, I'll tell him to take a look at it, see what's going on, OK?'

'Yes, I understand. But I . . .'

'What?'

'It's just, I felt it was my duty to inform you . . . I just thought I ought to let you know about it.'

'And so?'

'To be honest, whether the sound's coming from a radio, or some kind of shadow like you say, it's not actually that loud. Even if it were to switch itself on during a perform-ance, the sound effects would probably cover it up.'

The director's lips seemed to twitch into the merest hint of a smile, though perhaps it was only a muscle spasm.

'So you wanted to let me know that you've been hearing some mysterious radio broadcast, but that it's not disturbing you?'

'That's right.'

Before the director could say anything else, Ayami had hurried back to her usual spot in the library.

Late afternoon, with the sun bowing low in sky, the heavy orange radiance of the last light flooded horizontally into the building, but the world of the interior, where the lights were off, was already half sunk in darkness. The day's performance had been attended by five high school boys, a man who looked to be their form teacher, and a girl with a severe visual impairment, her eyes visible only as slender slits. The pupils kept fidgeting throughout the performance, and sprang up from their seats before it had properly finished. They practically flew out of the auditorium, yelling and shoving as they went through the glass door. The door swung back so suddenly it severed them from their shadows, which were left behind like dark ghosts.

The visually impaired girl was the last of the visitors to leave the auditorium. When she said goodbye, her middle finger brushed the back of Ayami's hand and then continued round to find a certain spot on the inside of her wrist. A brief gentle pressure, as though wanting to take Ayami's pulse. In that moment, Ayami was struck by the thought that the girl was inviting her along, in her own particular way.

The girl was oddly dressed, in a plain coarse-textured white cotton hanbok, which gave off the strong scent of starch. Her thick black hair was secured in a low ponytail, and rough hemp sandals poked out from beneath the hem of her skirt.

Ayami wasn't the only former actress who'd found herself in the role of office worker-cum-librarian-cum-ticket seller at the audio theatre managed by the foundation.

Before her, the position of office clerk had been filled by a string of other women who also had connections with the theatre industry, mainly as actors. The one who'd stuck it out the longest had stayed for three months; one woman had only managed three hours. No one had come even close to Ayami's two-year tenure. Frankly speaking, the job was tedious. Especially, that is, for young women more used to the excitement of acting. Here, the only people they ever saw were the few who came along to the audio performances, almost all high school pupils, university students or blind people. Her predecessors had all quit before their contract was up; perhaps due mainly to the fact that opportunities to meet men were so rare as to be practically non-existent. Not just any men, but the kind of men considered eligible by women whose youth and ambition sadly outstripped their limited means.

Ayami didn't know much about her predecessors. She'd never seen their faces, and didn't even know their names. All they'd left behind were a few ballpoint pens rolling about in a drawer, and a couple of sheets of notepaper bearing scribbled curses directed at no one in particular. She was equally in the dark when it came to the foundation that managed the audio theatre and paid her salary. Contrary to general assumption, she had no personal contacts there – that wasn't how she'd secured the job. Acting roles had become few and far between for her, to the point where she was even struggling to get parts at her repertory company; eventually, when the company itself had become embroiled in management difficulties, one of her fellow actors had introduced her to this place.

No one had come to meet her on her first visit to the audio theatre, and she hadn't received any guidance about where she was supposed to go. She'd entered the deserted auditorium and waited until someone appeared – the director. She'd been sitting facing the entrance, but still hadn't noticed him come in. He seemed to have materialised through a door made of light, which hovered amid the floating dust motes and shafts of sun. The director sat with Ayami on the auditorium's second flight of stairs, conducted a brief interview, and announced that she was hired.

The auditorium had neither a stage nor a screen. Instead, each 'performance' consisted of a pre-recorded script being played to the audience, using the sound equipment. This audience, never very large, sat on the sofas and stairs that had been installed around the auditorium. Accordingly, there were no actors, a title Ayami had relinquished now she was merely a run-of-the-mill office worker, occupied mainly with admin. Besides the auditorium, the theatre building contained a long lobby, a tiny library and, to the rear of the library, the director's office. Ayami spent most of her time in a corner of the library. Once a day, leading up to the evening performance, she sold tickets at the main entrance – these were extremely cheap, cheaper than a cup of coffee – and just before the start of the performance, she went into the auditorium and briefly introduced the play. The last thing she said was, 'OK, the play will begin now.' Very occasionally, someone would find their way to the library and ask to borrow a script or pamphlet of a recording, a collection of plays, an actor's autobiography, or even the recordings themselves, which were stored on CDs.

Ayami had tidied up all the loose ends of the various tasks assigned to her. She'd added up the ticket sales – not a job that took a great deal of time – checked the library's stock against the database, and posted the necessary documents to the foundation. All that was left was to lock the theatre door and put the key in the lower postbox. Her wages would be paid for that month, and then no more.

The library phone rang. Ayami took a moment to register that it really was the phone ringing, and not the mysterious radio, before she went over to the desk and answered the call. It was the usual enquiry, about the performance schedule for the coming week.

'There are no performances next week,' Ayami said. 'Today's was the last one; the audio theatre will be closed permanently from tomorrow.'

'You're closing?' They sounded genuinely shocked. 'Why hasn't this been reported in the papers?'

Perhaps it had. But all that would have been dealt with by the foundation's PR team, and Ayami hadn't been informed of any such notice being printed. Considering its low audience numbers, the theatre's closure was hardly as momentous an event as the person who'd telephoned seemed to think. At least, not so momentous as to warrant a mention in the paper.

The audio theatre is closing today, which means that from tomorrow Ayami will be unemployed. Of course, the foundation had made the decision several months ago, so she'd had plenty of time to find a new job. She'd been out of the business too long to get back into acting; in fact, that period in her life now seemed less and less real, especially once she'd recognised that she'd never been much in demand anyway. And then there was the unfortunate fact, only recently made clear to her, that her experience working at the audio theatre would be of absolutely no help in finding another job. This audio theatre, managed by the foundation, was the only one of its kind in Seoul. In other words, there was no job even remotely similar to hers; this was probably the case the world over, never mind just in Seoul. Ayami didn't have a single qualification to her name, anything that might have impressed a prospective employer. Nothing formally confirming her administrative skills or qualifying her to teach – nothing, in fact, that could even be considered an official document. Yes, she'd gone to law school, but had dropped out before the first term was up, meaning the hoped-for diploma never became a reality. She didn't even have a driver's licence.

In the downtime between acting gigs, Ayami had waited tables; unfortunately, this side job had been as much of a flop as her main career. The issue with waitressing was that she looked too tall. On top of that, whenever she took an order her face would wear the kind of expressionless mask more often seen in the theatre, and her movements, gestures, footsteps, all gave the impression of being unusually measured, done for dramatic effect. This apparent awkwardness rubbed off on the customers, and their discomfort was plain whenever Ayami approached their table. Most tried to disguise it by asking how tall she was, and her answer would invariably be met by an exaggerated raising of eyebrows and an insistence on examining the heels of her shoes. She always wore flats, without even the tiny sliver of a heel that most shoe manufacturers choose to add. Ayami's height was, on paper, nothing unusual, yet she appeared taller than she really was, as though she floated a few inches above the ground, a kind of optical illusion exaggerated during her shifts as a waitress, when the customers were almost always sitting down.

As she herself was keenly aware, Ayami's body was more suited to physical work than to the kind of customer-facing roles that rely on strong communication skills. Acting onstage, she believed, was a kind of physical work.

Knowing of Ayami's difficulties in finding a job, the director of the audio theatre had advised her to write a letter to the foundation. Given that her contract was with the theatre itself, a separate establishment, she'd had neither the need nor the opportunity to visit the foundation or meet anyone who worked there. All communication with the foundation went through the director. The only exception had been a couple of brief, dry telephone conversations between Ayami and someone from their art department – and those had only happened in cases of extreme urgency. The director thought Ayami ought to send her CV and a cover letter to the foundation's HR department. A suitable position might come up within the foundation itself, not right then, of course, but at some point, or else, though this was extremely unlikely, they might choose to invest in another non-profit cultural enterprise, or even end up reopening the audio theatre.

'You could do worse than get in touch with them,' the director told her. 'After all, you know they never advertise for new staff – it's all done through personal recommendations.'

But Ayami didn't take his advice. It wasn't that she didn't need a job, or that she didn't like the idea of working at the foundation. Though the director hadn't told her this in as many words, Ayami was aware that he himself had not been able to secure another job; at least, not one with the appropriate salary and status. If it had truly been the case that the foundation felt benevolent towards them, or that such feelings might be elicited by a mere letter, then the director would hardly have been experiencing such difficulties. And if the foundation wasn't willing to help him, then there wasn't much hope for Ayami. The director had received a top-class education, held a degree from a foreign university, and Ayami could see he had intelligence to spare. The only black mark on his CV, if there was one, seemed to be his time at the audio theatre, a non-profit enterprise where he'd commanded a staff of one.

Untroubled by clouds, the bright expanse of the evening sky spread out across the city. The entrance to the theatre building was a door at street level made entirely of glass. Hanging up the phone, Ayami gazed out at the gathering dusk, the red flare of the day's last light. Directly across the alley, a shabbily dressed middle-aged couple were looking over at the theatre. Every time a car drove down the narrow alley, the woman took a step back, onto the low paving slabs, where she balanced precariously until the vehicle had passed. Neither she nor the man seemed able to tear their gazes from what had caught their interest – the noticeboard by the entrance, where details of performances were posted.

For all intents and purposes they were an ordinary couple out for an evening stroll, or maybe primary school classmates who'd met up again after a forty-year gap. Every time the woman looked up and her unnaturally black hair fell back from her face, Ayami noticed pockmarks stamped here and there onto her dark skin. The man lifted a calloused hand and pointed at something on the noticeboard. Perhaps they'd realised that the final performance had been held that day. The woman was shaking her head, in what appeared to be a gesture of regret. Might they be my parents? This thought struck Ayami in a flash, then trailed off into the distance.

'It's strange,' she heard the woman muttering. 'How come we never knew this theatre was here? They need a proper sign, not just some notice stuck up like this. If you're not up close it just looks like a Buddhist temple or a cram school!'

When the man moved close to the woman and whispered something in her ear, she rested her head on his shoulder and giggled childishly. Ayami studied his slight frame; might he be her father, a fruit hawker who'd claimed a distant connection to the mayor of Seoul?

For a while, the couple seemed to forget the theatre that had appeared so abruptly in their lives.

They glanced up at the sky simultaneously.

The heat, the flat plane of the sky, were unchanging. There was no sign of rain.

'I wonder what's inside?' the woman murmured as she peered through the glass door, drawn to the place without knowing why. The man followed her gaze, though he had no knowledge of audio equipment to speak of, and precious little interest in anywhere calling itself an audio theatre. They seemed not to see Ayami on the other side of the door.

'Look, it says there's a library and an audio appreciation room. "Audio-appreciation room" – do you think that's the same as a music-appreciation room? No, but look at this, it says it's closed down! And we never even had the chance to take a look around.'

They started moving away, perhaps intending to head home, but almost immediately stopping again. They looked hesitant, as though wondering where they should go. Turning to face the man, the woman stared up at him with such intensity that furrows creased her brow.

'Darling,' she said, 'you won't really leave me like you wrote in that letter, will you?'

Her skirt fluttered like an old dishcloth in the alley's still air, exposing a pair of skinny calves corded with stringy muscle, pathetically small feet, and shoes that gleamed like new yet looked like cast-offs.

A single line of sweat trickled down from her hairline and over her cheeks. The smell of overripe fruit, cigarettes, damp laundry and fish wrappings wafted from beneath her skirt.

Rather than being some state-of-the-art space, the 'audio-appreciation room' consisted of a CD tower and a pair of headphones over on one side of the library. People would stand and listen to recordings before deciding whether to borrow them or not; nothing that really warranted such a grand title as 'audio appreciation'.

Might they be my parents? Ayami wondered again.

In the two years she'd worked there, Ayami had never taken a holiday, outside the one week in August when the theatre officially closed. For that week, when the humidity was generally at its peak, the foundation suspended all its various operations, disconnected its telephone lines, and gave every one of its employees the full seven days off. At this time of year, the city was like an animal being slowly smothered beneath a heap of steaming earth.

Crematorium smoke belched out from the hot asphalt covering every inch of soil, and from the enormous structures of concrete, iron and glass that towered into the sky, and whole streets became cratered balls of fire, with all kinds of animal matter – exposed flesh, skin, eyeballs, hair, sweat — burning up. Merely turning your face in a certain direction was enough for a storm of flaming arrows to inflict lethal burns. Thousands of stars exploded simultaneously. Meteors blazed, gas combusted, and the vault of the heavens was plastered with dark ash. All light was shut out in this dawn of night. But the heat didn't abate. At night, the viscous fibres knitting flesh together, underpinning the body's structures, slackened still further, fluttering and whirling around the edge of consciousness. The DNA sequences coding sleep's cellular identity unravelled, and dreams mingled with comatose states as cell membranes disintegrated. It was the time of the year when sleep was stretched thinnest, like oxygen at a high altitude. Yet it was also a time governed by a colloid of dreams in which gravity and density were most intense. In dreams Ayami would clutch a huge parrot to her breast, and in reality she would crawl into a non-existent bathtub brimming with cold water and fall asleep. The parrot dug its claws into her chest and produced a drawn-out shriek. The extremes of heat within the city, exacerbated by the artificially chilled air, were both sorrowful and transcendent. The midsummer metropolis was a temple of benumbed languor, the home of long-vanished, cult-worshipping tribes. Rarefied sleep sucked bodies into a burning crater lake choked with sticky flakes of black soap ash and honeycomb chunks of grey pumice. In cramped rooms unrelieved by air conditioning or even a fan, if you opened the window hot air heavier than a sodden quilt rushed in, clagging your pores like the wet slap of raw meat, but with it closed the oxygen would quickly evaporate, disappearing at a frightening rate until the air was filled with nothing but heat. Nothing but the ecstasy of ruin. August beds were pillars of hot-water vapour belched up from a bog, which held the memory of a female ancestor. An empire of agonising visions drifted up from its bubbling surface and floated over the city. These visions encroached on the dreams of its inhabitants. Air hotter than the heat of midsummer solidified into transparent bullets, penetrating one heart after the other, travelling between them with excruciating slowness. At every moment, the crystallisation of invisible wax ruptured skin and perforated flesh. Smouldering hunks of flesh. Mucous membranes ragged with burns. Breathing was a train headed for disaster. Every time the city dwellers fell asleep their bodies became cruelly soaked in sweat, like tinder doused with lighter fluid. They burned without flames through the long hours of the night. When the noonday sun was at its zenith, He drank a fridge-chilled beer, and She ate some cucumber. Now and then they switched on the boxy yellow radio, but all they ever heard was a weather report. The male announcer read the report extremely slowly, drawing out each monotonous syllable. Daytime. Air temperature. Thirty. Degrees. Celsius. Absence. Of wind. Absence. Of shade. Danger. Of fire. Thirty. Degrees. Absence. Of wind. Absence. Of shade. Daytime. City. Mirage. Scheduled. To appear. Melting. Of asphalt. And. Tyres. Absence. Of wind. Absence. Of cloud. Absence. Of mucous membrane. Danger. Of fire. Absence. Of colour. In the sky. And air . . . The candle left out on the windowsill had melted without ever having been lit; the wax collapsed pathetically under the sun's fierce rays, its shape suggesting the peculiar way love concludes. By the time the heatwave came to an end, nothing remained of the people but ash. They became fused into panes of glass: grey and opaque.

The previous year, when they'd returned to work after the summer holiday, the director asked Ayami how her break had been, and she replied that it had been very good. They acted as though they'd only just met, or didn't know each other very well.

Ayami explained that she generally spent her holidays with her wealthy aunt, who lived alone. Her aunt lived in South East Asia, a six-hour flight south, in a sandstone villa with a pool in the back garden. Early in the morning when Ayami went out to the pool, the surface of the water would be dotted with centipedes, spiders, even young snakes, alongside the unidentified dregs of black night. It never occurred to her to get rid of the insects, the various alien substances – she just dived into the water and started swimming. The water was a little chilly, but got gradually warmer towards the centre of the pool. Ayami's aunt rented the spare rooms out to summer holidaymakers, something only possible thanks to the Malaysian maid, Mimi, who did all the odd jobs (Ayami's aunt being over eighty). When Ayami felt inclined she would help Mimi make the beds and clean the rooms, but most of the time she spent lazing around, or going for strolls along the beach, feeling the coarse grey sand abrade the soles of her bare feet. Sometimes she would have a coffee and muffin at the McDonald's in the centre of town, and in the evenings head to the hotel's open-air bar, to sip a cocktail in the shade of the coconut palms.

'A wealthy aunt!' the director exclaimed. 'There's one in every family. I had one myself, though that was a long time ago. Wealthy, and also incredibly strict. She made us children walk on tiptoe in the house, so there would be "no unnecessary noise". There were three grand pianos but we didn't dare touch them, not even to tinkle the keys. For her, you see, even music was "unnecessary noise". She passed away a long time ago.'

Ayami showed the director a photograph taken in the city where her aunt lived. In the photo, Ayami is standing on the far side of a road, wearing a coarsely starched white cotton hanbok with no detailing or decoration. Her thick black hair is secured in a low ponytail, and rough hemp sandals poke out from beneath the hem of her skirt. Since the focal point of the photograph is not Ayami but the building behind her, its huge facade decorated with carved reliefs, the faces of the people in it have come out very blurred; it's unlikely that anyone would be able to recognise Ayami without being told. It's also impossible to tell whether the effect is deliberate.

'That building,' the director said, 'is that the municipal museum?'

'No,' said Ayami, 'it's the Hilton hotel.'

It was entirely down to the director that Ayami started taking German lessons. On her second day working at the theatre, the director had told her about a woman he'd known since university, who'd married straight after graduating, spent time as an exchange student with her husband in the same city as the director, but hadn't been able to complete her graduate degree. Now back in Korea, she didn't have a steady job and, after an abrupt divorce a while ago, urgently needed to earn some money. She'd hurriedly applied for a position teaching English at a cram school, but because she was older and didn't have any experience they were reluctant to give her a permanent position. The money she did earn there wasn't enough to cover her living costs, so she also gave private lessons at her home, not just in English but also French and German.

'One of Picasso's ex-girlfriends earned a living teaching French to American women in Paris,' the director said. 'It must be a classic step to take, one that transcends the ages.'

'Which girlfriend?' Ayami asked, but she'd already decided to take the director up on his suggestion and go for private German lessons (or French, it didn't really matter. At any rate, she had the sense not to expect that either would be of any practical use).

'Fernande Olivier,' the director said. The name meant nothing to Ayami.

The director's friend was small, slight, and unfailingly elegant, even down to her waist-length hair. Her face, though, was severely marked from a childhood bout of smallpox, making it impossible to estimate her age on a first meeting. Her skin was mottled, almost as though it had been burned. She had a strangely rolling walk, like a boat bobbing on gentle waves. She generally kept to the shadows, but when necessary would extend her right hand, its pale skin unmarked, into the light.

After the divorce was settled, she'd moved to an area three or four bus stops away from the audio theatre. Although the neighbourhood was technically downtown, its location up a steep hill and general air of dilapidation meant the rent was cheap. The woman occupied a one-room dwelling at the very end of an alley, where the sunlight never quite reached; it was a fair walk up the hill from the nearest bus stop. Ayami went there for a ninety-minute German lesson every day after work. Rather than have a conversation, they preferred to sit and listen to each other read from a book. Perhaps this was why, despite taking lessons for almost two years, Ayami's German showed scant signs of improvement.

The German-language teacher always made them a cup of tea. Hair pulled back from her forehead, she put her small brown feet up on a chair and sipped at the hot drink. She fished out the piece of lemon peel from her tea and rubbed it on the back of her right hand. The German-language teacher was like a shadow glimpsed through frosted glass. When she wordlessly reached out to pass Ayami her cup, her hand was a pale gleam emerging into the light of a mid-summer evening. On one recent occasion, their reading was interrupted by a radio located somewhere inside the room.

'What's that sound?' Ayami whispered.

'The radio.' The German-language teacher's voice was not dissimilar to the one that had disturbed Ayami.

'Why switch the radio on just now?'

'It must have come on by itself.'

'Well, switch it off again.'

'I can't, it's impossible.'

'Why?'

'The radio . . . the switch is broken, you see. So it turns itself on, and then turns itself off again.'

'Just pull out the plug.'

'I can't, it's impossible.'

'Why is it impossible?'

'I . . . because I'm frightened of electrical sound. It's frightening, like gas, or knives, or lightning.'

'Ah, I see.' Ayami looked at the German-language teacher and nodded. They both returned to their tea. Beads of sweat formed on their foreheads. The room's sole window opened directly onto the wall of the dead-end alleyway, thereby serving absolutely no purpose, and the humid air collected in the house's dark interior, so dense you could almost have swept it up with a broom. The scent of yellow sphagnum wafted from the fishbowl – the goldfish had died long ago – to mingle with the sweet smell of the mould blooming on the lowest part of the walls. The house might as well have been a temple for the worship and propagation of tropical heat – heat that swelled like a bog within those four walls. Certain agonising apparitions were bred in this place, a mental state known as monsoon disease. Given that the narrow room had neither air conditioning nor a fan, if you opened the window hot air heavier than a sodden quilt rushed in, clagging your pores like the wet slap of raw meat, but with it closed the oxygen would quickly evaporate, disappearing at a alarming rate until the air was filled with nothing but heat.

But Ayami probably wouldn't be able to visit the tropics this year, because the theatre would be closing down before the usual holiday period, and the possibility of her finding another job before then looked slim.

'A while ago an unidentified node – that was the doctor's term – developed in my left breast,' the German-language teacher whispered, her voice seeming to come from within a semi-concealed black mirror. There was a moment's silence. 'It's actually quite common for people my age,' she added. Ayami asked if this was true. If, that is, it was really just a node, something trivial, nothing to worry about.

'That's right,' the German-language teacher said, nodding. 'It's a common thing. But it wouldn't feel real to a young person like you.'

Ayami had never once thought of herself as particularly young; now, with unemployment staring her in the face and not much time left before her twenty-eighth birthday, the description seemed especially false.

'In life – there are – wounds that – like leprosy – slowly – eat away – at the soul – in solitude.'

The German-language teacher read from the book, her voice toneless and devoid of all emotion. The lessons progressed with them each reading a page per lesson from a novel in German. Their current text was *The Blind Owl*.

Lost in thought, and with her finger resting on the cover of the guestbook, Ayami suddenly turned her head. A silhouette was visible on the far side of the door; a man, standing with both hands pressed against the glass. Having decided to stay behind for a while at the end of her working day, Ayami had locked the main door after the last of the audience members – the visually impaired girl – had left. If the man had tried to get inside, he would have found himself thwarted. How long had he been there like that, hands on the glass, peering inside? Ayami went over to the door, the look in her eyes asking what was the matter. But the man remained silent, seemingly unable to understand her.

The man's pose – legs slightly parted, head lowered, both hands resting on the glass – recalled that of someone praying with their whole body, or whose strength had been utterly exhausted. His gaze was directed towards the floor, so it was difficult for Ayami to get a look at his face. She could see his bushy eyebrows though, thick and black like two furry spiders. Then, having noticed Ayami, the man raised his head a little. The two of them gave a start of surprise as they realised how close they were, then stood motionless, gazes locked.

The man's eye sockets were like sunken caves in his gaunt face, and his lips were dry. The capillaries webbing the whites of his eyes were alarmingly distinct, and now that it was late afternoon the shadow of a beard darkened his jaw. All in all, though, his face was perfectly ordinary, the kind of face commonly encountered on the bus or subway, the kind of face Ayami had come across plenty of times. The man stood as still as a bronze statue. Even his eyebrows were rigid. He just bored into Ayami with his gaze.

Ayami froze. Unconsciously, she inched her hands up to the point where her outstretched palms mirrored those on the other side of the glass. A tremor shuddered through Ayami's heart. She felt her body being seized by a shockingly intense emotion, one she couldn't identify. An emotion surpassing will and consciousness.

I am emotion, she heard something inside her whisper, speaking in her stead. I am nothing but emotion.

What's the matter? Ayami's lips moved to form the words, but no sound came from her mouth.

Then the man spoke, his voice low but strong.

'I have to come in! Why have I been driven out?' He didn't appear drunk, but Ayami saw a strange madness in his eyes. Startled, she took an involuntary step backwards, all the while wondering how she was able to make out the man's low voice so well, given the thick glass door that separated them. In a voice that she didn't know was trembling, she explained the theatre had closed for the day. Perhaps, she thought, the man was able to lip-read, though of course there was no way of knowing. Just in case, she enunciated the words as clearly as possible, saying, 'We're closed now, I'm telling you we're closed.'

The man clenched his fists and waved them about as though he was going to batter down the glass door.

'I won't go quietly,' he whispered, his voice almost inaudible. 'I'll kill you all!'

The strange man had Ayami confused with someone else, or else it was the audio theatre itself that he'd come to by mistake. He clearly had absolutely no intention of leaving, glaring at Ayami as he heaped abuse on her, until two security guards eventually appeared, ready to drag him away. By this time he'd worked himself up into a real passion, the whites of his eyes now more crimson than white, threatening to explode at any moment. Unable to meet that crazed stare any longer, Ayami looked away. How old is this guy? she wondered. Thirty-two? Fifty-six? Was this a temporary bout of insanity, had some recent occurrence sent him mad, or had he always been this way? His light brown jacket and trousers hanging loosely on his gaunt frame; his checked shirt with the top buttons undone; his staggering steps and furrowed brow; the wordless signs of misfortune imprinted all over his body; all the markings of a failure; his heavy Adam's apple bobbing perilously up and down; his desert-dry gunmetal skin; his shining eyes, dangerous and venomous. Might I know him after all? Ayami no longer trusted her own memory.

And the man's blue trainers. His whispering, clearly discernible despite the intervening glass. The blood filigree lacing his eyes, his sandpaper lips, that intense yet inscrutable emotion. An emotion shredding the fibres from her heart, pulverising it, yet strangely enough with a calming effect, conscious thought sifting slowly down into a bottomless abyss.

I am emotion.

If either of them had been paying attention to their surroundings, they might have noticed a green car go by. The driver was a middle-aged woman wearing a colourful summer dress and with what looked like a towel around her neck. She'd had one hand on the wheel, the other held a phone to her ear. Out of the corner of her eye she'd caught a glimpse of the theatre's glass door, the man outside kicking up a fuss, but that had nothing to do with her.

A man carrying a kitten in a birdcage pressed himself against the opposite wall of the alley to avoid her car. He was a preacher, a well-known figure in this alley; he went around surreptitiously stuffing pieces of paper bearing Bible verses into people's pockets, so he'd been mistaken for a pickpocket and arrested more than once. While she waited for the lights to change at the end of the alley, the woman driving the green car took her hand off the wheel and raised a bottle of water to her lips. Still with the phone to her ear. Against the regular growl of the engine, the hum of the air conditioning.

'Slowly, my fingers slip inside your trousers. They're still warm. I've had them stuck between my wet swollen lips, you see. Down there between my legs, a warm peach drenched in syrup. Take off your belt. Hold on, not your trousers. I'm still just caressing your dick, getting the feel of it, picturing it. It's nice that way . . . we can take it slowly . . . now close your eyes and imagine me, your dirty whore, down on her knees in front of you.' And a light groan.

Ayami gazed in wonder at this woman's multitasking – driving and phone sex both required a great deal of concentration. She quickly turned away though, alarmed by the prospect of further obscenities from the woman, who seemed to have genuinely aroused herself. The two security guards grasped the man by the arms and succeeded in hauling him out to the car park.

Even after the man was gone Ayami stood in the same spot for a while.

The phone in the library rang.

It was the German-language teacher, who asked how Ayami was before saying, 'I'm taking medication, quite a lot, actually. But I don't need to worry about the cost; it's a new wonder drug, and I've been chosen as a test subject for the trials, luckily. So far I've had no side effects, apart from the fact that I'm sleeping a lot these days.'

For those few moments, while the teacher was speaking, Ayami thought she might actually be able to read the lips of someone she couldn't see, on the other end of a phone line. But then she remembered the crazy man, and the thought vanished.

'He came here,' Ayami said.

'He? Who?'

'That man, the salesman who used to go to your house from time to time.'

'He must like you – didn't I say so? But he isn't a salesman, Blind Owl.' The German-language teacher generally chose a name for Ayami culled from whichever novel they were reading. She found Ayami's real name much too strange, and not at all to her liking. She'd told Ayami that her real name made her uncomfortable and that, where possible, she wanted to avoid having to pronounce it. She had also asked not to hear it pronounced: 'Whatever you do,' she said, 'just don't say "Ayami". And the same goes for calling me "Yeoni".'

'You're a young woman, Blind Owl, and a beautiful one. If he went to see you . . . well, it's not unusual for one person to yearn for another. Did he buy you flowers?'

'It wasn't that kind of visit – the opposite, if anything. He threatened to kill me . . . no, to kill us.'

'You must have misheard. Or else it was a joke, and you misunderstood.' The German-language teacher's voice was gentle, dismissive. Ayami tightened her grip on the phone.

'I didn't mishear. He was right there on the other side of the glass door. I didn't open it, of course. What kind of person jokes about killing someone?'

'He's just a bit different . . . but he's not violent. He certainly wouldn't harm someone for no reason. And if you didn't open the door, how could you have understood everything he said?'

'I just − I just did. I could see him saying it, I mean. And I heard it, too, very clearly.'

'Well, I suppose it's possible.'

'My thoughts are all over the place right now, so it's difficult to remember. The thing is, though, I've studied lip-reading, so I could make a good guess at what he was saying. Might he be angry because we didn't let him join our German lessons?'

'I've just remembered something he told me: that you and he have known each other for a long time. A very long time.'

'That's not true.'

'But that's what I heard . . . at least, that's what I remember. And not that you were simply acquainted . . . something more intimate than that. An unusual intimacy, that has existed for an unusually long time . . . I could be misremembering, though − perhaps a side effect from the pills.' A brief sigh followed in place of any further explanation.

Reading the lips of someone you can't see, someone on the other end of a phone line − perhaps it was an illusion, after all.

'Anyhow,' the German-language teacher said, returning to her original reason for calling, 'I guessed you would still be at work, and I have a favour to ask.'

Ayami said she would be happy to help, as long as it was within her power.

'Do you think you might have some spare time tomorrow morning?'

Ayami asked what was the matter.

'Someone I know will be arriving at the airport very early in the morning. Could you go and meet them? It's their first time in Korea.' The German-language teacher paused, then, with a sudden earnest intensity, said, 'There's no one else I can ask, Blind Owl.'

The messages in the guestbook were nothing out of the ordinary, but someone had skipped to the very last page and drawn a picture there. It was a simple sketch, clean pencil lines delineating the form of a boat – small, low, long and nimble-looking. There was also a boatman, standing very upright. The whole thing appeared to be more a symbol or glyph than an attempt at naturalistic representation, but it also demonstrated a certain dignity and proficient draughtsmanship. The boatman could have been either a man or a woman with long hair and a slight figure. And the fact that s/he happened to be standing in a boat didn't necessarily make her/him a boatman. After all, it wasn't an oar they were holding in their hand, but a bird.

The bright liquid darkness of a midsummer evening was seeping between the blinds and slowly collecting inside the auditorium.

Ayami stood up and walked across the stage, moving just as she had when she first learned to swim: both arms spread and each hand with its fingers pressed together, swaying in a manner both careful and hurried, a cross between a fish's lateral propulsion and the way seaweed dances in the current. The 'stage' didn't exactly warrant the name, marked as it was by nothing other than a small table placed in front of the audio equipment, used only when a guest speaker came to give a talk on audio drama. Standing to attention at the theatre's entrance, Ayami would introduce the title and author of the play, concluding with: 'OK, the play will begin now.'

On the stage (the small space immediately in front of the table) Ayami lies supine with both arms outstretched, her palms facing upwards. The empty seats regard her in silence. Ayami is completely still. Her eyelids cover her pupils, her hair covers her face. Is she dead? Once more, that whispering voice trickles from the hidden radio.

Weather forecast. For. Sailors. At sea. A south-easterly. Waves. 2.5 metres. Further out at sea. A south-westerly. Some. Cloud. To the south. A faint. Rainbow. Localised. Rain showers. Hailstorm. North-easterly. 2. 35. 7. 81 . . .

Ayami has an appointment for 8 p.m. at a nearby restaurant. Recalling this, she wakes from her false death.

Ayami arrives at the 'blackout restaurant' at exactly 8 p.m. The sun has set, but it is not yet completely dark: that shadowy border region between day and night. The dazzling lights from the shops brashly crowd the streets, like mobsters in garish suits. After the chill confines of the air-conditioned subway car, Ayami is flushed with feverish heat. Slow-forming clouds clot the sky like lumps of ash. As she enters the long, narrow alleyway where the restaurant is located Ayami is met with a dense wall of hot air.

When you step inside the restaurant you find yourself in a bright, open waiting room. The low hum of music drifts in from an adjoining bar. First, you must confirm your reservation, and then the staff at the counter will take your order. You can have a drink at the bar before your meal, and there's a closet for bags and bulky outer clothes, which would get in the way once inside the restaurant itself. The wooden door leading into the dining room remains closed but you can go through once you've ordered your meal. They hate to admit it, but most people feel themselves tense up when they stand in front of that door. Some are frightened, some even cry. After all, this is the door to another world, to another form of sensory experience.

There are two rules to bear in mind: the first is that the use of any kind of luminous device is forbidden. This includes torches or anything with an LCD screen or smoking paraphernalia such as lighters or matches, and even cigarettes with their potential to be lit. Incense sticks, by the same logic, are also taboo. The second rule is that, once inside, you mustn't get up and wander about. If you did, you'd end up bumping into the other guests and getting in the way of the waiters. If you have to use the bathroom, or want to go out for a cigarette, the proper procedure is to call for the guide, who will be waiting nearby. It's their job to lead the guests around.

Having been informed that the director was already inside, Ayami entered the restaurant. As soon as the door was opened for her, pitch-black darkness smothered her vision as though Indian ink was poured over her eyes. The darkness had an almost tangible density, crowding in around her and pressing itself against her eyes. She had to push her way through that absolute darkness, using her own mass to physically displace it, which made it a thousand times more difficult to move around. The constant hum of the air conditioning, low bursts of laughter and murmured conversation, the clink of tableware — all the usual sounds associated with a restaurant were present, but lacking their visual counterparts. The darkness was absolute. Not the darkness of a cinema after a film has started, and which is bound to be mitigated by light belched from the screen, or by cat's eyes guiding you down the aisle. Here there was only utter darkness, darker than the inside of one's eyelids, a colossal coalface rearing up in front of Ayami, which she had to crawl up with the aid of a ladder.

'Ms Kim Ayami?' The voice was that of a female guide, still just a girl from the sound of it.

'Yes,' Ayami replied. 'That's me.'

She felt the guide's strong fingers clasp her wrist and her hand brush the back of Ayami's, her middle finger touching the inside of Ayami's wrist. A brief gentle pressure, as though wanting to take Ayami's pulse. The girl gave off the scent of harshly starched cotton. The guides and waiters who worked at the restaurant were all blind, or at least had a severe visual impairment. To them, the interior of the restaurant was fundamentally no different from the exterior world. Ayami let the guide lead her to her table and sat down.

'Today's performance was *The Blind Owl*.' This was the first thing out of Ayami's mouth.

'I know,' the director's voice answered. 'It's been the same all week.' That voice was dry and slightly cracked, with an uneven intonation. Not, at any rate, the voice of an actor.

'Some high school students came with their form teacher,' Ayami said. 'Apparently they have to write a piece on their impressions by next week.' In the darkness, Ayami's voice insisted overwhelmingly on its own identity. It was a corporeal voice. Just as, in the light of day, people can't help their gaze going to a beautiful woman, in the darkness they pay more attention to the voice. They accept the mystery of seeming to feel the other's gaze on their skin. Their guide brought soup and a basket of warm bread, its smell unmistakable. Though it wasn't their first time here, the waitress still followed procedure and explained the table settings to them.

'Each guest has their plate directly in front of them. The fork is to the left, the napkin and knife to the right. There are two glasses at one o'clock, and the basket of bread is at eleven. The glass for water has a wave pattern etched into the surface, and the one for alcohol is smooth. The spoon has been placed at exactly twelve o'clock.'

'In the dark I always end up gripping the spoon harder than I need to, it's a difficult habit to kick.' The director's voice said this as soon as the girl had left. It laughed, then asked, 'How was closing?'

'All fine.'

'Ah, that's good. Nothing out of the ordinary?'

Ayami recalled the man who'd been causing a disturbance, but decided it wasn't so important and that she might as well keep it to herself.

'I don't grip the spoon too hard, but . . . I find it difficult not to be able to read your lips.'

'You mean you generally lip-read first, before listening?'

'Well, there are times when I can read someone's lips without actually being able to see them. Though I can't understand how it happens.'

'Some kind of sensory illusion, is it?' The director's voice was warm and friendly. 'How will you get on in the future, Ayami? Do you have any plans?'

'Nothing concrete yet. I've tried various places, but I haven't heard anything positive back.'

'Did you write a letter to the foundation, like I suggested?' the voice asked.

'No.' Ayami shook her head, but stopped as soon as she realised the pointlessness of such a gesture.

'Do it before it's too late, it'll be a help. I'm serious. You're a talented young actress and you've done great work at the theatre, so if a new position comes up with the foundation's cultural arts team there'll definitely be an opportunity for you.'

'I haven't been an actor for two years,' Ayami responded with a light laugh. 'And my work at the theatre hasn't been connected with performing arts, it was just simple work that anyone could do – you know that better than anyone!'

'Once an actor, always an actor, right? Even if you can't get an acting job and have to support yourself through other work, nothing will change that fact. The way I look at it, it's a vocation, isn't it? Rather than just an ordinary job?'

'Vocation only applies to work that nourishes the soul.'

'And everybody has a soul, no?'

'Well, what is a soul, exactly? What kind of soul?'

The starters arrived. Ayami guessed that she was eating pickled red pepper, dried clams and fresh paprika. They devoted themselves to chewing slowly, in silence.

After a while Ayami opened her mouth to speak: 'I'm thinking of looking for a temporary position.'

'Temporary? You mean like something part-time, that pays by the hour?'

'That's right.'

'You aren't thinking of working at a restaurant again?' the director asked doubtfully.

'I might, but not right away. Last week I had an interview for a short-term administrative position at a university; I haven't heard anything back yet, which means that's a no. Before I came out this evening, the German-language teacher asked me to do her a favour: I might be interpretreting for a poet visiting Korea, and doing some secretarial work for him. But it's not confirmed. The poet's going to make up his mind when he gets here.'

'Ah yes, I remember hearing something about that.'

'But I . . . I didn't think I'd be able to interpret so I turned it down, but she said it's not conference interpreting so it should be fine. I told her I didn't mind finding him somewhere to stay, helping him choose a place, et cetera.'

'What's he coming here for?'

'To write, apparently.'

'But why Korea?'

'I wondered about that, but all I got was that he "just happened" to choose Korea. There's no official event for him to attend – in fact, nobody else even knows he's coming.'

'Maybe he's coming to see Yeoni. A personal visit, I mean.'

'I thought that, too. But then why would she want me tagging along all the time?'

'She'll probably be starting chemotherapy soon.'

'She told me she's just taking pills!'

'Pills will only do so much.'

'She said she was trialling some new wonder drug she was so lucky to be taking!'

'Did she say anything specific about this new medicine?'

'No.' Ayami shook her head vigorously but, again, pointlessly. 'She said it was a secret. She said she'd signed a written pledge to keep it absolutely confidential until the product came on the market. She can't hold them responsible for anything, either. Not any side effects – nothing. In fact, she shouldn't even have told me that.'

'Anyhow, even if she does start having chemotherapy, it doesn't mean she won't be able to see anyone.'

'I don't know. But if the poet's coming here to write, he must intend to stay for a little while.'

'And so . . .'

'. . . he'll probably see Yeoni every now and then.'

'Didn't Yeoni once work as a temporary secretary for a famous writer, a long time ago, when she was studying abroad? He wanted to write a novel about Korea, so she looked up various documents and translated them for him. But then the writer changed his mind, so the book never saw the light of day. He was pretty famous, and for each new project he'd pick a new secretary who fitted the theme.'

'Really? A temporary secretary – perhaps that's the proper name for the work I'll end up doing. But I can't think of any theme I'd be especially suited to.'

'That'll be for the writer to decide. When would you start?'

'Early tomorrow morning so, really, you could say later tonight. That's when I have to go to the airport.'

'You know, I met a poet today. It's an odd coincidence, now I think about it. Though to be precise, I would have to say I met "poets", plural.'

'Today at the foundation?'

'Yes. Today at the foundation.' Perhaps the director nodded. 'A while ago they announced a programme to support the work of various poets – but you probably already know this. Today was the launch event. I had nothing to do with it myself, but I'd dropped by to see someone from the arts team and they asked me to stick around.'

'I never realised the foundation was involved with that kind of thing.'

'I assumed you knew . . .'

'How would I, when it's nothing to do with my work, and I don't know anyone at the foundation? I've never even been there.'

'Right, you told me; I keep forgetting.'

'So, did the poets all have their own secretaries?'

'Secretaries!' the voice exclaimed, its laughter sounding cold, mocking. Just then, the main course arrived. Ayami picked up the strong smell of roast lamb.

'Secretaries!' the voice repeated. The director's cutlery clattered against the plate; he seemed to be prodding at his fish, worried about the possibility of bones. 'Try some, Ayami. I'd never seen so many poets in one place. It was the first time they held this kind of event. Of course, I've caught a glimpse of a famous writer now and then. At a public reading or a lecture, that kind of thing. I'm probably more familiar with their photographs in the newspapers. Though when I was studying abroad I crossed paths with Ko Un while he was visiting Europe. We even exchanged a few words. I doubt he would remember me now.'

'And did Ko Un have a secretary with him?'

'Possibly,' the voice replied, somewhat curtly. 'There was one woman always by his side but apparently she was his wife, not his secretary. So today, when I saw all those poets gathered in one place – there must have been dozens of them, all in the same room – I couldn't tell they were poets at first. Because more than half of them . . . it's not easy to put into words, maybe this was a subjective impression, but more than half, most, in fact, if I'd passed them on the street I would have taken them for someone self-employed who'd gone bankrupt after the IMF crisis, wandering around with no home and no family. I wouldn't have been all that surprised if they'd asked me for a little money, just to buy something to eat; that was how they looked to me. But . . .

no, it wasn't their appearance exactly, it would be more precise to say that they followed a physical mould, which made me feel a certain way towards them.'

'I can't imagine it.'

'Well, that's how it was; at least, if I'm to be honest, it's the impression I had.'

'Do you mean it was like a gathering of hipster poets?'

'I've never heard that phrase used to describe a particular group or movement. I know hippies used to be a thing, though; is it something like that? I've no idea what kind of poetry they write, but from the looks of them I'd have to say they were just ordinary, run-of-the-mill poets.'

'Sometimes, on my days off . . . I wear scruffy clothes . . . like ripped jeans or a shabby T-shirt with the neck all stretched.'

'Ayami, I'm not talking about anything as literal as that!'

'Maybe poets have just never been concerned about dressing smartly? I've never met any writers, apart from a playwright at the theatre, ages ago. He always wore ordinary jeans and a T-shirt. There was nothing to distinguish him from the actors. Now I think of it, he did act sometimes as well. And he didn't even have long hair. Well, no longer than the actors, I mean. Anyhow, he was no different from us. But, judging from books and films, a lot of artists like to look distinctive, so I think I understand what you mean.'

'No, Ayami, you've misunderstood me. As I said, the issue wasn't what they were wearing. They all seemed to have chosen outfits they hoped would make them look very conservative, very civilised. As they did, in most cases.'

'What was the issue, then?'

'Well, describing a strong impression in a handful of words is more their territory than mine – poets, that is. I wasn't born with that talent, unfortunately. But I'll give it a go. When I first saw them, I was struck by how old, how grey, how bleak they seemed, almost without exception. It was so pronounced that at first I felt shocked. It wasn't just abstract, it was a physical sensation coming from their bodies, as though they were emitting particles. When they gathered in the lecture hall even the lights seemed to lose their radiance, becoming dull, making the room gloomy. I don't actually recall whether they were especially old, biologically speaking. What I do remember is their faded grey hair, their bent, almost hunched backs, their listlessly bowed necks, the glinting spectacles shielding their myopic eyes, their fatigue-inflamed irises, the harsh scent of cheap fabric, fake leather bags, facial muscles stiffened into a mask of long-suppressed frustration and sadness, overlaid with an innate ugliness, bodies all either fatter or more stunted than average, all kinds of external symbols of poverty, swollen feet threatening to burst from shoddy shoes, beads of saliva dangling from shabby lips . . . They, they were like dead people!'

'If I'd become a poet . . .' Ayami murmured dreamily. 'If I had . . . of course there's no way I could be, I've neither the ability nor the motivation, but if I had, even if my external appearance was no different from what it is now, perhaps I would have looked to you like those you saw today. In that case you would have described me as an objectively hideous woman, a woman with a pockmarked face, a person incapable of being loved, who seemed dead even when she was living; as a person who draws on that negative energy to produce their poetry.'

'Ayami, you misunderstand me! There could be a dangerous misunderstanding here. None of this has anything to do with you. You're not a poet. There's no need to identify with them. You're still young, healthy and beautiful. The future belongs to you; why make such a frightful substitution?'

'I'm not so young. And I'm certainly not beautiful. And as for the future belonging to me, is that a line of poetry? It sounds so unusual.'

'Don't worry too much about finding another job. As long as you have the resolve, it will all work out, though it may take a little time. Take my advice, and write a letter to the foundation. They'll be sure to respond.'

'It's not despair over my job prospects that's making me pessimistic. It just came over me all of a sudden. Though, in fact, ever since the German-language teacher . . . ever since Yeoni postponed our lessons because of her illness, I've found myself becoming depressed every now and then.'

'Yeoni will get better. Her health will recover.'

'Why would she have taken an unknown, experimental drug in the first place?'

'She must have believed it would cure her. And, of course, it was free.'

'Oh, yes,' the director said after a pause, 'I was talking to one of the poets, Kim Cheol-sseok, and he gave me a collection of his poetry.'

'Kim Cheol-seok?'

'No, Cheol-sseok, Kim Cheol-sseok.'

'That can't have been his real name, can it?'

'I asked that, and he said it was a pen name, something he'd made up.'

'Did he explain what it's supposed to mean?'

'Apparently it's the sound of earth being poured onto his coffin.'

Ayami didn't laugh. Her attention was concentrated on making careful forays with her fork, until she finally succeeded in spearing a piece of lamb and bringing it to her mouth.

'He also said,' the director's voice continued, 'that he'd never once managed to convince another person of anything. Whenever he spoke to anyone, their response amounted to nothing more than the world tossing a shovelful of earth onto his grave. Which meant that by this point in his life, he was buried deep, very deep; he laughed for a long time after he said that, bleating like a goat.'

The guide approached without a sound and then asked: 'Shall I bring dessert?'

Ayami said yes – she had ordered walnut ice cream – but the director now wanted only a cup of coffee. The sound of the air conditioning, which had filled the room, abruptly shut off. Not a minute passed before their skin became clagged with particles of stifling heat. Ayami felt droplets of sweat form behind her ears and trickle down the nape of her neck.

'A power cut,' a voice said, when the air con was heard to start up again. 'There must have been a sudden spike in electricity usage.'

The director's voice picked up where it had left off. 'That was the last thing he said to me – I left almost immediately afterwards. And someone pulled the door tightly closed behind me, though it had been open the whole time. But before it closed completely I sensed that the room was suddenly plunged into darkness. I say sensed, not saw, because I was facing the other way. As though all the lights had gone out; no, as though the lecture hall itself had disappeared . . . I couldn't explain it . . . I suppose they might have been going to use a projector, but still . . . it was as though all those silent elderly poets had been sucked into the shadows, taking their suspicious body odour with them, vanishing into thin air. Could I have been talking with myself the whole time, sitting among three-dimensional images whose forms were obliterated the moment someone slammed the door behind me, without anyone having turned to watch me go? The traces of this imprecise notion lingered in my mind.'

'What kind of poetry does Kim Cheol-sseok write?'

'I don't know – I had a meeting after the event, and left his book there. I only realised after I got here.' There was a sigh as he said this, but seemingly not over the book. 'When I returned after the meeting, the terminally unconvincing seemed to have left long ago: the lecture hall was deserted. But I stood in front of the door for a long time. I couldn't bring myself to leave.'

'Why?'

'Because I'd realised that I, yes, I who had pitied them was pitiful myself, a pitiful person who'd also always failed in convincing others. In other words, I was one of them.

I hadn't been with the wrong people, or in the wrong place, at all. They were a hallucination of myself, so I couldn't help but despise them. I'd been talking with the ghosts of myself, perhaps the ghosts of my future. I just hadn't realised it!'

'Is it really so important? Being convincing?'

'Oh yes, it's important. That's self-evident. As for how important, everyone has to judge for themselves.'

'Mightn't it be a . . . poetic expression? What people call metaphor, or metaphysical expression? Words like Max Ernst's *objets*, for example, flying about in the air around us. Abstract objects clothed in the material. Like the gap between word and image, like how we are here while our ghosts could simultaneously be wandering in some northern desert. Perhaps the ability to convince others, or the lack of it, isn't as meaningful as language itself . . . the difference between someone who receives love and acknowledgement from others and someone who doesn't, it might be important in the world of words and concepts, but is it really so decisive for ourselves, for our egos? After all—'

'Yes?'

'After all, as you said, we aren't poets. Using language to convince is not our calling. If someone wants to pour earth over our faces, we can just avert our gaze and keep on as we were. Like the herders of the Altai. That actually is how we live, you know, every day.'

'But doesn't that leave us incredibly isolated? If we can't convince a single person, not anyone at all, and if no one has any interest in our graves, you say we can simply turn away and go alone into the wilderness. Without knowing where it is we're going. We might have to spend our days with only the sheep and stars to gaze at. The stars die and are born again, and it must be the same for the sheep, mustn't it? You'd say that the world is unchanging. But if we lived like that, and eventually lost even the sad consciousness of our own inability to convince, that would be incredibly lonely, Ayami.'

'So we have to convince others because we're lonely?'

'Because loneliness is failure. I, at least, have had obligations I couldn't fulfil. Like preventing the audio theatre from closing . . .'

'That's beyond the power of any one person. It was the foundation's decision, after all.'

'Not only that; ultimately, I even failed to convince my wife. I couldn't undo a single one of the many knots that had formed between us. Those knots will keep dragging me along, shaping my life . . . as though they themselves are my life's essential form. That's right, my wife doesn't want to see me. She hates me more than anyone else in this world. I understand her hating me. She says that it's because of my incompetence and my silence, but the real reason is that I married her, and dragged her into my life. Her hatred is becoming something irrevocable. I am powerless in the face of it. And this is how I will be defeated by my own life, how it will triumph over me at the last, as a part of the unchanging world.

'Do you remember the quote, that though a person's fate can be endowed with its own meaning, a hundred destinies are less significant, and what we call the individual history of thousands and hundreds of thousands is meaningless?

'That's true loneliness. Ayami, I'm a very ordinary type of person. Not a man like those you see in Max Ernst's paintings. My whole life, I've only ever walked well-trodden paths. I've been afraid of being alone. Thinking about it now, it's not clear whether it is loneliness or meaninglessness that I've truly feared. Even so, I've always failed to get people to agree to things. That smell of the suburbs, of people whose jobs have mainly been sinecures, I'm well aware of how it pervades me. And, to give a more concrete example—' the director's voice broke off briefly. 'As you wrote in your letter, in the end you will leave me, won't you?'

Someone bumped into Ayami and muttered an apology, muffled and inarticulate, as though they had spoken into their scarf or collar. When they moved past the faint scent of cat came from their clothing. Or it might have been the smell of a pine marten or badger. Ayami was sitting alone in the outdoor smoking area. A withered, neglected hydrangea was tangled against the wall. Ayami was watching her own huge shadow wavering on the wall.

Though she had few memories of her childhood, one event protruded sharply from the oblivion like the wreckage of a sunken ship. It was of the village pharmacist going missing. The pharmacist had been a young man, too depressed and taciturn to be close to anyone, and one day he had disappeared. He'd left behind a letter saying that he hated society and was converting to Buddhism. His young wife, whom he had married less than six months previously, was pregnant. There was also a pharmacy assistant involved. The assistant, a man of thirty who, unlike the pharmacist, was sociable and had a good head for business, taking care of practically all of the day-to-day management, helped the young wife after the pharmacist abandoned her, and arranged the disposal of the business. He also – though this was clearly illegal – sold off the medicines on the sly. But a little while later a rumour began to circulate. It was said that rather than going to the mountains to become a monk, the pharmacist had a nail driven into the crown of his head while he slept and died without anyone being the wiser, and that his corpse was hidden in the space between the ceiling and the roof. And that the child his wife was carrying was not his. Though the police came by and turned the house upside down, even tearing off the roof, they discovered no trace of anything suspicious. One day the pharmacist's assistant left the village alto-gether, along with the pharmacist's wife. No one knew where they went.

'Penny for your thoughts, Ayami?' The director came over and put a cigarette between his lips.

'I was just wondering who gave me my name.'

'Ah, that you wouldn't remember. When I named you, you were still just a tiny baby.' The director smiled at his joke. Absent-mindedly sticking her hand into her pocket, Ayami's fingers touched a piece of paper. She fished it out and read aloud what had been written on it:

'There is not much time left, so from now on he who has a wife must live as though he does not, and he who has sadness must live as though he does not.'

'That is truly the best news of all – as welcome to my ears as a blast from the angelic trumpets,' the director mumbled, his voice emotionless, betraying no hint of laughter.

'It's a message from the pastor. I didn't even notice him slip it into my pocket; his fingers are light as a pickpocket's.' After a short silence, Ayami spoke again. 'I just had a thought – at some point, if the opportunity comes up, I'd like to write a fairy tale.'

'There's a time and a place for a dream like that, but what you need right now is a regular income. Otherwise, how are you going to pay next month's rent?'

'Have you forgotten? I'm to be the foreign poet's temporary secretary . . .'

'But that's only temporary! And this so-called poet, apparently coming from abroad, has provided no contract stating how much you'll be paid and when. What if he arrives at the airport, looks around, says, "Hmm, I don't fancy this place after all, I'd prefer to go elsewhere," then what'll you do?'

Ayami shrugged. 'I hadn't thought that far ahead.'

'For God's sake, I'm telling you this because I don't want you to end up in the same category as me.'

'What category?'

'The category of invisible people.'

'And what does that mean, invisible people?'

'People who can't be successful, who can't convince others.'

'Don't talk like that, people would laugh to hear you put the two of us in the same category. And not for the reason you think – quite the opposite. In any case, you've convinced me.'

'Not if you end up leaving me.' The director brought his face close to Ayami's. 'But even when a woman says she'll stay, that isn't down to my convincing them, so the end result is the same.'

His lips could be seen to move. What was visible were not the words themselves but segmented syllables that his lips produced one after the other.

'Have I ever told you that I used to be a bus driver?'

'No, you've never told me that you used to be a poet.'

'In that case perhaps I already said that at one time I was not only a playwright employed by a theatre company but also an actor-director? And that a very long time ago I was a village pharmacist?'

'No, you haven't told me that you were none other than my father, who was a fruit hawker.'

The director's lips moved sluggishly.

'And you haven't forgotten what I wrote in the letter, that I made the decision to leave you a long time ago, far longer ago than you imagine? So in that sense, we've already parted?'

At that, Ayami's skirt fluttered like an old dishcloth in the still air. The porcelain dish doubling as an ashtray fell from the edge of the table to the concrete, breaking into two pieces with a loud crack. The movement of Ayami's skirt exposed a pair of skinny calves corded with stringy muscle, pathetically small feet, and shoes that gleamed like new yet looked like cast-offs – but in the shadows of the dark yard, all of this remained unknown. The director's eye sockets were like sunken caves in his gaunt face, and his lips were dry. The capillaries webbing the whites of his eyes were alarmingly distinct. Now late at night a dark blue shadow spread over his jaw. The whites of his eyes were wholly crimson, and those eyes gleamed with a burning intensity, forcing Ayami to look away. The wordless signs of misfortune imprinted all over his body; all the markings of a failure; his heavy Adam's apple bobbing perilously up and down; his desert-dry gunmetal skin; his shining eyes, dangerous and venomous.

Ah, do I know this man? Ayami was struck with a feeling of vertigo. Instantly she was swept into the past.

The young Ayami was walking along a road when she came across a small blue pebble and picked it up; beneath the pebble, a deep, gaping hole led to the world on the opposite side of the mirror, which existed simultaneously with this one (she remembered someone having told her this). On the far side of the hole another Ayami was living in another world. In that world there was a city and a window, a river and a bridge with a car driving over it, there was a temple and in the temple yard an old woman with a severely pockmarked face was scattering white grains of rice for chickens. Ayami was her future self or her past self. And she was both, existing at the same time. In that other world, she was both the chicken and the old woman. That was the secret of night and day existing simultaneously. Ayami discovered this through a single movement, bending down to pick up the pebble. And, remembering this simultaneous existence more vividly than she remembered herself, became unable to remember anything else.

Two hours later, Ayami opened her mouth. 'In any case, I have to go to my teacher's house. There's been no answer, even though I've phoned dozens of times.'

'Might she have gone on a trip somewhere?'

'Even if she had, she'd still answer the phone. She told me to call again tonight, and that she would tell me in more detail about the poet I'm meeting at the airport. Apparently they met entirely by chance, sitting next to each other on a train in Europe.'

'I'll go with you.'

They hailed a taxi, which took them through the deep night streets. As though photographed at a slow shutter speed, the city lights were elongated into multicoloured ribbons, streaming past the window.

As the alley leading to Yeoni's was too narrow for the taxi, they were dropped off at its entrance and walked the rest of the way. The alley was pitch-black and the houses were hunkered down, unmoving, uninhabited, as though the buildings themselves were dead. The unpleasant, humid stench given off by the dirty concrete walls lingered even at this late hour. Television laughter, families whispering, the smell of a late dinner cooking over a fire, the clamour of a marital spat, the shrieks of children and drunks' slurred yells; there was no trace of the basic yet depressing scenes common to poor neighbourhoods.

The unlit streets lacked even the tiniest kiosk.

They held hands as they walked up the hill, pushing through the sticky air.

'So, what sort of fairy tale do you want to write?' the director asked, as though the question had just occurred to him.

'I want to write a mysterious, secret story with stock characters.'

'Stock characters?'

'A blind princess and a brave knight dressed as a swan, a wicked dragon and magician,' Ayami elaborated, her breathing laboured.

'I've never read a fairy tale,' the director retorted, 'so I find them difficult to imagine. They've never been my thing.'

'What kind of stories do you like?'

'Stories of adventures I'll never be able to have. Of pirates, bandits, robbers and thieves. Like Robin Hood and Peter Pan.'

Finally they arrived at Yeoni's home. The lights were off here, too. They stood for a moment, catching their breath. 'Apparently the people in this neighbourhood are being relocated. It's been chosen for a "model district" project, to improve residential environments,' Ayami explained to the director.

'Then she's moved out already?'

'There's no reason to think that. If it was going to be today, she would have told me.'

They pushed open the front gate and stepped into the tiny sunken yard. Not only was it extremely dark, but it was crammed with all sorts of odds and ends, so they had to fumble their way forwards using their hands for guidance. The director knocked on Yeoni's door.

There was no answer. The lights did not come on, and there was no sign of human activity.

Widening her eyes so she could see better, Ayami noticed a family of dead cats, laid out side by side between empty cardboard boxes in a corner of the yard.

'Try opening the door,' she whispered. 'She always leaves a key under the flowerpot.'

The director found the key and used it. The door led straight into the kitchen. Water was dripping from the tap into a tin bucket, the sound echoing off the concrete ceiling, amplified in the damp darkness. Ayami found the light switch and flicked it, but nothing happened.

'There must be a power cut in the whole neighbourhood,' the director grumbled. They passed through the kitchen into the other room.

There was no one inside. Again, they had to grope about. Once her eyes grew accustomed to the darkness Ayami saw the blue medicine bottle on the table. She checked that the boxy yellow radio and *The Blind Owl* were still in their respective spots on the shelf and in the bookcase. The candle was in its usual place on the windowsill. On the table next to the medicine bottle was paper and a pencil, as though Yeoni had been in the middle of writing a letter; a book lay open at the head of the bed. Ayami read the title in a low voice.

'*Where do we come from? What are we? Where are we going?*'

'What did you say?' In the darkness, the director's voice seemed to stammer.

'It's from the collection of plays she'd chosen for us to read after *The Blind Owl*.'

They went outside and stood at a loss. Had Yeoni gone out? Ayami suggested they ask next door. Providing there was anyone living there. She remembered that the landlord and their family had lived on the opposite side of the yard but a glance through their dreary, curtain-less window revealed a bleak scene: the living room furnished by a broken floor lamp, metal coat hangers, clothes, and an umbrella the size of a seaside parasol. It was smoky, faintly stinking, stationary, the smell of unidentified metal, impoverished, dark, heavy, unclear, stifling, in a state unknown to anyone, already dead for a long time, and more than anything else unbearably hot.

'Let's get out of here.' The director grasped Ayami's arm. 'I saw a police station down at the bottom of the hill. Let's ask there.'

Retracing their steps, everything was the same as it had been on the way up. Only now there was a middle-aged woman sitting alone on a bench in the darkness; they hadn't seen her earlier. The woman was clutching a fan and had her thin underskirt hitched up to her waist. The alley was so narrow they were forced to pass right in front of her. The woman, who looked to be a little over fifty, was absorbed in fanning her naked crotch with straight vigorous strokes. The darkness pooled between her thighs was extremely deep. She raised her severely pockmarked face towards them.

Behind her, a wooden sign bearing the hand-lettered word 'accommodation' hung from a low gate.

The lights of the police station were visible on the corner at the bottom of the steep path, as the director had said. He and Ayami went inside. Two policemen in identical uniforms, one young and one old, were lounging askew on their chairs. When Ayami and the director got close, they realised the policemen were asleep, though their eyes were still half open. Both wore long jackets with wide sleeves, unsuited to the muggy weather. By their feet was a birdcage and inside it a kitten was sleeping. The clock on the wall had stopped at twenty-three minutes past seven. Beneath the strange lighting the officers' complexions almost matched the grey-green of their uniforms.

The director tapped on the table with a finger. Without fully opening his eyes, the young policeman raised his eyebrows enquiringly. Ayami and the director explained the situation, and asked whether it might be possible to put out a missing person announcement. The young policeman asked if the missing person was a family member; they replied in the negative. Very well, the policeman said, how long might the person in question have been missing for? He didn't sound convinced.

'I spoke to her on the phone earlier, but there's been absolutely no contact since then, and when we went to her house just now there was no one there.' Ayami made sure to state their case carefully. 'Besides, the whole neighbourhood is oddly dark, and there's no sign of anyone at all.'

'It's only natural for a residential area to be dark and quiet at night. Especially in a neighbourhood like this, where most people will have been out working since early morning, meaning they also go to sleep early. You say you went to your friend's house and she wasn't there; are you sure? She might have been asleep and not heard the bell, or just not wanted to open the door in the middle of the night. Besides' – he gestured towards the clock – 'it's almost one in the morning; coming here talking about how strange it is that the lights are all off and the neighbourhood's quiet as the grave, and then mentioning a missing person, that puts us in an awkward position, you know.'

'But, our friend's house really was empty . . .' Ayami glanced at the director standing a step behind her. She hadn't decided whether it would make any difference to tell the policeman that they had actually gone inside Yeoni's home. But the director remained mute in the shadow of the wall.

'She must have gone out somewhere, then,' the young policeman said, not bothering now to conceal his lack of interest.

Throughout all this, a drunk wearing a mask lay sleeping like a stone, every bit as motionless as the kitten.

When they left the station they found themselves facing the grey expanse of a double-lane highway. A white bus passed along the otherwise empty road, its interior brightly lit. Inside the bus several women were grouped around a large table, each reading a book, and in the darkest corner of the back seat a monk was sitting with his eyes closed.

Ayami and the director walked the streets aimlessly. An ambulance siren pierced their ears, though they couldn't see the ambulance itself.

'There must have been a car accident,' Ayami said eventually and, as she spoke, the shrill sound dwindled into the distance, swallowed by the darkness.

They stood for a while staring at the empty road.

'Now I think about it,' Ayami said, 'maybe we jumped to the wrong conclusion. Yeoni might have gone to the hospital. She didn't say so on the phone, but . . . maybe she was feeling unwell.'

'Which hospital?'

'I don't know.'

'You're right, that must be what happened. Well, that's a relief.'

They crossed the road via a footbridge. The floodlights were unlit and there was no one else around. Looking down, a shoal of night fish appeared, glimmering silver in the current of the night. The footbridge bobbed like a boat on the waves. The very bus that had gone by a few moments earlier was now speeding along the overpass opposite them, and looked as if it were trying to reduce the night to ashes by swiftly circling a specific section of the city, like a carousel horse rotating on a fixed orbit.

They were at the centre of the vast rectangular city; it just so happened that all its inhabitants were simultaneously asleep. They did not know the whereabouts of the absent one. The city's name was 'secret'. Every window was closed, dark, silent, invisible; every window was itself the city, quietly meditating. The square in front of the train station hung before them like the surface of the moon, with a black statue rising from it. Is that a train passing by in the distance? There is no wind, yet the flag is taut in the air. A chimney soaring into gunmetal clouds, the square, a night train standing on the waiting line, the statue of a nameless general, and rows of empty arcades.

The cry of the white owl, white lightning cutting through the air, wagons with black coverings, and the figures of dead people were nowhere to be seen.

'It's like being in a dream,' Ayami said, still standing on the night footbridge. 'Where are we going?'

'We're going to buy some wine,' the director said confidently. 'We have to make a toast.'

'What are we celebrating?'

'Your German-language teacher Yeoni's health, and our new journey!'

'That's nonsense.'

'Yeoni will be all right. She's just gone to the hospital!'

'She'll be all right, but you know perfectly well that there's no such thing as "our new journey". And where will we buy wine at this hour?'

'This is the station, there's bound to be a 24-hour store.'

Unbelievably, no sooner had the director finished speaking than they saw a brightly illuminated convenience store in the station arcade. A beautiful yet lonely light, like a small candle flickering in a clearing surrounded by dark forest. Each item for sale shining as though with a light of its own, gleaming white behind the glass wall. Ayami heaved a sigh and smiled at the director.

'It's like you're a magician.'

'Take your time,' he shouted back at her, dashing down the steps on the other side of the footbridge, 'I'll go ahead and choose the wine!' He ran across the square, arms swinging back and forth.

'Wait for me!' Ayami shouted after him. 'Don't be in such a rush!'

Skidding to a halt in the middle of the square, the director raised both arms above his head. 'I don't want this good feeling to dissipate! And you have to go the airport soon, so there's no time to lose!' His black hair had blown back from his white forehead and the enormous shadow of him stood in the empty white-paved square. It looked like a living statue.

After waiting to watch Ayami step down from the footbridge, he turned again and ran straight towards the light of the store. Ayami followed, walking slowly.

After the figure of the director had disappeared, seemingly absorbed into the store's bright light, Ayami spotted a man walking across the same road she and the director had crossed using the footbridge. Her immediate thought was that he was the crazy man who had come to the theatre earlier that day. But there was no way that could be right. Not that it would be absolutely impossible for that same man to appear here, but because Ayami could not recognise someone only in the form of a shadow, which was all the vague darkness disclosed.

The man walked over the subway ventilation shaft at the edge of the square. He wore thin summer clothing, and walked with both arms held away from his sides, twirling his empty hands. He walked over the yellow lights set into the paving stones. He walked alongside the white railing of the flower bed, and he walked into the shadow of the statue on the tall plinth. Ayami stopped. Was the man merely out for a night-time stroll? The man also stopped. They stood unmoving for a few moments, regarding each other from a distance.

Ayami had the feeling that the man was waving to her. Somewhat hesitantly. Ayami's sight was not good. She was unable to precisely make out the small movements of the man on the other side of the square in this vague night. All of a sudden, the man changed direction. He had turned round and was walking back towards the road. As though his intention had been only to greet Ayami.

Just then the white bus came barrelling back. Faster and faster it raced along the road, before miraculously coming to a halt just in front of the man – still more surprising was the lack of any sound, either of brakes being hastily applied or of friction from the tyres. But when the bus came to a stop, the man's body had already fallen to the ground; a black lump like a huge animal stretched out to its full length. Inside the brightly lit bus, several women were grouped around a table, each absorbed in a book, and in the furthest corner of the back seat a man wearing monk's robes was sitting with his eyes closed.

Ayami had to close her mouth with her hand. She believed she had just seen the man die. The door of the bus opened and out came the monk and the driver, the latter wearing a uniform – it wasn't clear what kind, but it featured an enormous hat. They picked the man up and carried him on to the bus. Ah, they're taking him to hospital. Ayami found this thought reassuring, though the initial shock had yet to pass away. The women on the bright bus were sitting stock-still, each with her gaze riveted on her book. They were reading an illustrated *Kama Sutra*, its vivid colour images of bodies contorted into unusual positions. Perched on the roof of the bus was something Ayami hadn't been able to make out before – a single white crow.

2

One humid evening, Buha went to the riverside to cool off.

At the riverside was a wharf where couples on dates could rent a boat. Though Buha was alone, he asked to take a boat. He had nothing else to do.

After putting on a life jacket he rowed out to the middle of the river. Not five minutes had gone by before his whole body glowed with heat. The surface of the water sparkled yellow in the evening sunlight. An unbroken stream of cars passed over a nearby bridge, carrying commuters home from work. Each time invisible lightning split the air, the water beneath the metal-and-concrete bridge splashed and churned.

Buha's boat had drifted near to the bridge when a man plummeted from that bridge into the river. The man flailed, reflexively trying to swim, his limbs jutting above the surface like broken pieces of wood. But the current was too strong.

Acting on instinct, Buha jumped into the river and swam to the man as the latter began to sink. As soon as he was close enough, the man thrust up his arm and caught hold of Buha's life vest. Supporting the man's neck with one hand to keep his head above the water, Buha tried to swim back to the boat, but it had drifted too far away. The evening sunlight streamed straight into Buha's face, forcing him to keep his eyes closed. The man who had fallen into the water thrashed still more violently. Glittering grey scales of river water rushed into Buha's mouth. He tried to jerk his chin up, but the man had Buha's neck in a desperate chokehold. Buha gave up on the boat and swam to the riverbank instead. It occurred to him that even if he did make it to the boat he wouldn't be able to pull himself up into it. The riverbank was far away. They themselves were so small, and the river looked much too wide. On the footpath a dog was barking at them. A white dog, its long fur almost concealing its face. The sky was overcast with dark clouds, and the air was muggy. Above the water a white hot-air balloon was bobbing along. In a basket suspended beneath it was a heavily made-up clown. From the basket hung a placard that read, 'I am lonely. Say hello to me.' When the children strolling by the river waved at the balloon, the clown waved back, with one hand stuck to his forehead. The balloon's white silk bore the word PEACE. Very slowly, it flew over the heads of Buha and the man.

All of a sudden they were very close, the man's eyes watching Buha. But his pupils were unfocused. The man's eyes were like sunken caves in his gaunt face, and his lips were dry. The capillaries webbing the whites of his eyes were frighteningly distinct. Just then, Buha sensed that the man's limbs, though trembling, were starting to stiffen. The man was unmoving, his arms and legs now limp. Buha made sure the man's face was turned upwards, and saw that the man was in fact an adolescent, still in the first flush of youth. Foam was coming from the youth's mouth, along with a strange groan; his eyes were only half open. Now able to swim far more easily, Buha soon made it to the riverbank, where several people out for a walk helped haul the two men onto dry land. Buha sucked air into his lungs in ragged breaths. His heart was pounding fit to burst. The small group of bystanders examined the youth collapsed at their feet, turning his body over. If he were dead, all Buha's efforts would have been for nothing. But the youth was breathing. 'He's having an epileptic seizure,' someone said.

While the passers-by continued on, leaving Buha and the youth lying on the bank, Buha adjusted his wet clothes and trudged over to the dock. He was barefoot, having left his shoes in the boat when he plunged into the water. He tried to find his ticket for the boat rental, struggling to think how to explain why he'd come back without it, but the people who ran the rental service had already gone out in another boat to rescue the one Buha had abandoned, having witnessed the whole scene unfold. They handed Buha back his ID with no questions asked. The woman who had been holding it for him also handed him a towel, which Buha used to dry himself off.

Buha wanted to be a poet. It had been his dream for several years when he was in his twenties. But he had never written a single poem. In fact, he'd hardly even read any. To him, poetry was filled not with language or letters or rhythm, but the image of one particular woman. A woman who really was a poet. And who was beautiful. Especially when she smiled, and it seemed as if all the world's light radiated from her eyes and lips. Though Buha had only seen this smile in a black-and-white photograph printed alongside a newspaper interview. The black-and-white pixilation made the poet woman's face appear as if dappled by shadows, the black spots like nails driving into her skin, making sunken holes; the white spots liquid pouring from those same holes. It had been twenty-something years since Buha had seen the poet woman's photo in a newspaper. He had dreamed of being a poet ever since. Since the poet woman was a poet, he too naturally wanted to be one. He had no intention of buying a poetry collection, attempting to write a poem, or attending any literature classes. He simply wanted to be a poet. Buha saw no contradiction whatsoever in the gulf between dreams and reality. (Otherwise why would we have to distinguish between them, calling a dream a dream and reality, reality?)

It wasn't as if he thought of her constantly. After a few years had passed, she came less frequently to his mind or to his dreams, and then a whole year might go by without him picturing her face. Buha remembered the poet woman with the greatest intensity whenever someone asked what he dreamed of being, and as he grew older such occasions grew fewer and further between, one could almost say ending completely.

An employee of the export division of a textile company, Buha went on many business trips, generally to South America, a journey that unfortunately could take more than twenty-four hours. He once went to the Chilean port city of Valparaiso to meet a Korean fabric trader who was setting up a business there, and when he was eating breakfast alone in a cafe near his hotel, a woman came up to him and said, 'Hello, my name is Maria. Where have you come from, sailor?' Maria did not have a pretty face and her skin was too dark for Buha's taste, dark brown like seaweed, the backs of her hands were rough as a hedgehog's spines, and she lacked even a single front tooth, yet she had the talent of putting a person at ease, talking to them in a voice that was calm, gentle, kind and child-like.

'What's your name?' Maria asked in a sing-song tone.

Buha introduced himself as Kim.

'Kim, is it OK if I sit with you?' When he told her to go ahead, she said, 'Just buy me a Coke, I won't bother you for long.' Maria's childish voice stirring some sympathy in him, Buha bought her a Coke as she requested.

They left the cafe after an hour; Maria took his arm as if it were the most natural thing in the world to do, but Buha, embarrassed, pulled away. Maria said her home town was in the northern desert. Her father had worked in an oil-sands mine, and after he drank himself to death Maria had come to Valparaiso to work in a beauty salon run by her aunt. Business at the salon was slow, so her aunt also earned money as a psychic, albeit not a very good one. Buha deliberately sped up, walking several steps ahead, but Maria kept babbling on, making an effort to keep up with him. Afraid of attracting the notice of someone he knew, Buha turned around and, without saying a word, handed Maria some money. As he did so, his business card dropped to the ground, and as Maria bent down to pick it up, Buha turned and fled at a speed Maria had no hope of matching.

A few years later, after quitting that job, Buha and two colleagues who had left with him set up a company of their own, trading fabric with China. This new work had him coming and going between Seoul and an unheated apartment in Shanghai, but though business was good early on, five years later there was nothing for it but to let the company fold. They had little cash left after settling their debts, returning Buha to the state commonly known as penury. This was two years ago. Had it not been for a small sum of money he had inherited from his parents, his circumstances would have been dire. By then, he had almost completely forgotten about the poet woman. Perhaps because he had stopped asking himself what he dreamed of becoming.

Buha managed to get a temporary job at a pharmaceutical company, where he packaged and delivered blue pills. It was part-time work, on-demand. Though not necessarily down to financial reasons alone, it was also around this time that Buha split up with his second wife. One night she shook him awake and said: 'Call me by my name.'

He said her name.

'Not that name, I mean the name you gave me.'

Buha asked her what she was talking about.

'I just figured it out. Why we've always been so inexplicably drawn to each other.'

'I don't know what you're talking about,' Buha said, adding that he hadn't been the one to name her. Obviously.

Until he'd met her, he'd never known a woman with that name. He told her that as far as he was concerned her name was both new and unique, like a second moon that rises over the desert. That her name was to him a singular event in this world.

But she shook her head. 'We're too close to each other. A very long time ago, we were far closer than we now remember. And so each time you enter my cave your face looks like that of my father, my older brother.'

Buha was now wide awake. Blanching, he sat up and said he didn't know what she was talking about but, regardless, there was no way they could divorce. Various other reasons aside, he had given up too much to marry her. And because he was no one's father, and no one's older brother. And he was absolutely not the one who had named her.

'You're not?' his wife asked in a half-sunken voice. 'Then who are you?'

'I'm your husband.'

A while later he found out that she was having an affair with her boss.

The blue pills he delivered came in white-glass bottles unlabelled apart from a sticker at the bottom of each one bearing the name and address of the recipient. Buha had been delivering the bottles for some time when he happened to hear from one of the company nurses that the pills could 'also alleviate the symptoms of an epileptic seizure in the temporal lobe'. They had not yet been given manufacturing approval, but their effectiveness was clear.

'You say they "also" alleviate the symptoms of temporal-lobe epilepsy, so what were they developed for?' he asked the nurse.

'Oh, originally they were a kind of painkiller; they can be used as a local anaesthetic in non-invasive operations, and can suppress inflammation. But apparently they also block excessive activity in special nerve cells in the brain. It's outstandingly effective, they say. It's just that it can't be publicly acknowledged. There's a lot of lobbying against established pharmaceutical manufacturers but, I mean,' the nurse continued tentatively, 'not many people are aware of the exact effects of the main ingredient in whatever medicine they take. And even if you're aware, it doesn't mean all that much. Hospital prep rooms are full of pills that look exactly the same, and they get mixed up more often than you'd think.'

At nights, there was a woman Buha sometimes called. One day, he found her business card stuck under his windshield wiper, like the promise of a secret assignation. Written on the card was a telephone number and the words, 'Please call freelancer Yeoni.'

Each time he called, the automated message said: 'This conversation is charged at x won per minute. If you do not wish to be charged then please hang up now.'

Buha received a letter forwarded from a former colleague. He was surprised to see that it was from Maria in Chile, addressed to the company where he'd worked.

Buhakim, you must remember me, right? It's Maria, from the northern desert. We met in Valparaiso. You were a generous and kind person. I'm writing a letter to the address on the business card you gave me.

My circumstances have become very bad since we met. My aunt died in a traffic accident and the salon was claimed by loan sharks. I got a job at a different salon, but I had to quit that, too. Salons are constantly closing down, so it's difficult to find work. Even when I have a job the pay is still terrible. I'm still being paid the same as when we met, sometimes even less. So the thing is, could you send me just a thousand dollars? If a thousand's too much, five hundred will do. For the rent. When are you planning to come to Valparaiso again? I'll be happy to see you when you do. If you could send me a thousand dollars in the meantime, or even just five hundred, I'd be as happy as if my mother in heaven had come back to life again.

Maria

The same summer he received the letter, Buha was travelling back from one of his deliveries one day when he encountered the poet woman at a bus stop. Even though he had never seen her in real life, and though he hadn't seen her black-and-white photo in a newspaper since his college days, in other words more than twenty years ago, she looked almost unchanged. She was tall, which surprised him, not that he'd been able to estimate her height from the photo in the paper. If anything, he'd guessed she would have a small, naturally slender frame. The poet woman standing in front of him now wasn't smiling. To Buha, her unsmiling face was the most unfamiliar thing about her. He had never seen her that way before.

She was wearing a white blouse and a thin, cotton summer skirt whose blurred colours made it look like a dishcloth. The skirt fluttered each time she took a step, exposing skinny calves corded with stringy muscle, pathetically small feet for such a tall woman, giving the impression that they had been torn from another's body and hastily stuck on hers, and shoes that gleamed like new yet looked like cast-offs. She was a carrying a black, imitation-leather bag over her shoulder and a book in her hand. The book had a blue cover, and its title was in a language Buha couldn't read. He thought it was probably German, which he'd learned a little of at school, a long time ago, but had since forgotten. Buha made a great effort to suppress the desire to approach the poet woman and ask why she wasn't writing poetry any more. (Since he hadn't seen any articles about her in the papers, he had long assumed that she'd stopped.) You have a reader waiting anxiously for your poetry! There shouldn't be any need to confess upfront that he hadn't read a single one of her poems.

And with neither motion nor sound, like particles of sand being drawn body and soul through the narrow opening in an hourglass, Buha was pulled in a direct line towards a specific moment in the past.

*

Clasping the book to her chest like a student, the poet woman stepped into the narrow alley lined with houses, and Buha followed as though sucked in by her wake.

The summer sun was setting over enormous tangles of telephone lines, the flat old concrete roofs, bundles of laundry and bunches of roses, chickens being raised on rooftops. They walked on and on, following the old alleyway as it snaked up the concrete hill, where poor families lived crowded together.

They became wet with sweat simultaneously.

Their bodies were a dozen metres apart, yet they exchanged breath as though they were one. The poet woman disappeared inside a low concrete house near the top of the hill.

Though Buha neither read nor wrote poetry, he did sometimes draw. His mother had been an artist. His father, a civil servant, had retired from the Ministry of Culture, and was around fifteen years older than his mother. He was a bigot and conservative in thinking and appearance. On afternoons when she had been starved for conversation Buha's mother used to say to her young son: 'What an artist really needs is not a husband but a sponsor.'

Though they came close several times to divorcing, Buha's parents stayed together until the end of their lives. When he lived with them he had felt a vague sense of compassion for his mother but now he hoped his father, who had lacked self-expression at home, might at least have had a lover. Though it would not be a mistake to call his father authoritarian, his authority had no ego. An autocrat, yet one who could not rule over anything, and whose autocracy had no ego to it. He lived then died like a yellow ghost.

Late one autumn his mother did not come home till lunchtime after spending all night at her studio. She didn't move from the sofa the whole afternoon; instead, she just sat and examined her paint-stained fingers. Though this occurred to Buha only now, his mother had also taken home-delivered medicine for the last few years of her life. She had said they were simple headache pills. Buha couldn't say he had ever understood his mother, but he had learned how to sketch by looking over her shoulder.

'Try drawing a ship,' his mother said first.

Buha drew a ship in the guestbook.

In the oldest form of prehistoric cave art, a ship is an ideogram signifying 'I'.

Buha didn't have a single memory of his mother laughing. He recalled instead that she enjoyed reading the bestselling series *Jokes*. These were the only books she read. Now and then she would even read a few pages out loud to him. For example:

An old couple in their sixties are walking by the seaside when they come across a gourd. When the husband opens it a single stem of smoke escapes, swiftly assuming the form of a genie. The genie says, 'Thank you so much, I've been trapped in this gourd for a thousand years because of an evil magician's curse, and now you have set me free. As a reward, I will grant each of you a single wish; speak them.' The wife speaks first. 'I want to have a two-storey house with a garden. A house with a swimming pool and a tennis court, with a view of the sea from the bedroom on the upper floor.' 'Nothing easier,' the genie says, and gives a shout of concentration. At that, a marvellous two-storey house with white marble walls appears right in front of their eyes. Now the husband feels brave enough to reveal his own desire: 'I don't need anything else, only to live with a woman thirty years younger than I am.' The genie shouts again, and the husband immediately ages thirty years.

The house into which the poet woman had disappeared was low, with not much difference in height between its roof and the road, since the yard was sunken. Plastic bags filled with rubbish were piled against the walls, themselves blackened by an unidentified shadow. Everything beyond the rusted dark red gate was vague and gloomy. A strong scent of mould was concentrated in the yard.

It was the strangest of coincidences, but Buha had just been on his way back from delivering medicine to a woman living in this very house; in this unusually dark house, where she lived in the shadows. When the door opened the woman's contours were revealed as though in a dim mirror. A fossilised face of a second woman, blended with darkness and shadow, flitted from one window to another. In the late-afternoon midsummer light the woman's right hand appeared white and distinct. The weather forecast on the radio was faintly audible. Since a single bottle held a fortnight's worth of pills, under normal circumstances he would not have returned to this house for another two weeks.

Were the two women mother and daughter? Might the poet woman also take the same medicine?

On his way home, Buha stopped by a bookshop and looked for the *Jokes* series. He remembered his mother reading *Jokes 3*; the shop owner recommended the latest title, *Jokes 5*, published some time ago now.

'Would you listen while I tell you something?' Buha said to freelancer Yeoni that night.

'Of course I'll listen to you. And you listen to me, too, please. After all, isn't that why you called?' Yeoni's soft voice flowed out of the receiver.

'I called because I wanted to tell you about the book I've just read. I'd be grateful if you would listen and then give me your frank assessment as to whether it's funny or not.'

'OK,' Yeoni responded, as though nodding her head on the far side of the receiver, her voice sincere.

'A Japanese student called Suzuki transfers to a school in the US. During the lesson, the teacher asks, "Who said 'Give me liberty or give me death'? Anybody?" The students avoid the teacher's gaze and the classroom lapses into silence. Suzuki alone raises his hand and shouts triumphantly, "Patrick Henry, Philadelphia, 1775."'

'What a good student,' Yeoni put in, 'memorising all that.'

'There's more. Praising Suzuki, the teacher tells the rest of the class to follow the example of this foreigner who had diligently studied American history. At that, someone at the back of the classroom is heard to mutter under his breath, "Damn Jap."

'The teacher gets angry and shouts, "Who was that? Who said that?"

'Suzuki raises his hand and says, "General MacArthur, 1942, the Battle of Guadalcanal."

'A different student exclaims, "Ugh, this makes me sick."

'This time, before the teacher has even asked the question, Suzuki comes out with: "George Bush, 1991, eating sushi with Tanaka in Tokyo."

'Finally one enraged student gets to their feet and curses Suzuki openly. "Suck my dick."

'Suzuki's cheerful answer: "Bill Clinton to Monica Lewinsky, 1997, the Oval Office of the White House."'

Yeoni was silent.

'So, is it a good joke?'

'Well . . . it's not unfunny but, how can I put it . . . you can smell the artifice. It's too obviously intended to stir up anti-Japanese feelings among Americans. In other words, it sounds less like a joke and more like political irony. A joke is just meant to make you laugh, but this is like something written by a journalist with an axe to grind. A knife disguised as a pen. Jokes aren't just humorous, they also deliver us from the weight of reality, right?'

Buha was disappointed. He had discovered this story in *Jokes 5* and had hoped that when they finally came to share their first conversation, it might make the poet woman smile again.

'And the part at the end about Bill Clinton? To me that's the worst. It ought to be erotic, but it's not. Some sexual innuendo gives a joke its finishing touch, I think. But this . . . it sounds like a political attack, which renders the people impotent.'

Despairing, Buha changed the subject.

'I got a letter from a woman called Maria, whom I met just once in Chile around a decade ago, asking for a thousand dollars.'

'Is this another joke?'

'No. It's true.'

'Was she a woman who sold her body?'

'Not necessarily, but . . . something similar.'

'And you haven't met or had any contact in the meantime?'

'That's right. I had no reason to go back to Chile.'

'This is better than that other joke.'

'It's really true. I had no contact with Maria. Never mind contact, I can't even remember what she looks like.'

'I've just remembered that I read a similar episode in a novel, a long time ago.'

'Which novel?'

'A novel by Jorge Amado. He was a Brazilian writer. A communist.'

'The nation is the people and the people do not die. Do you know who said that?'

'I don't. Amado, by any chance?'

'Abraham Lincoln, apparently.'

'Where did you read that?'

'In this book, *Jokes 5*.'

After the call was over Buha put into an envelope the five hundred-dollar bills he'd withdrawn from the bank just before it closed that day, and sealed it carefully. He wrote Maria's Valparaiso address on the outside.

Buha enjoyed deviating from his fixed route to watch the poet woman. Many women liked taking classes, and the poet woman was no exception: she was learning German. After work she went to a house in a poor hilltop neighbourhood. Sitting with his back against an unusually low wall, Buha was able to hear her hushed voice coming from inside the dark rooms of the house, where she would read aloud from a book. In that house there were two women. The customer to whom Buha periodically delivered medicine, and the poet woman. Buha could not tell what sort of relationship they had. Since the customer woman always remained in the shadowed interior that was like a frosted mirror, only wordlessly reaching out a white hand to take the medicine bottle from him, her face remained unknown. It was as if one woman was the shadow of the other. When they read from the book at the same time their voices could not be distinguished.

The book the poet woman read from every evening was *The Blind Owl*.

She worked in a place called an audio theatre. It had very few visitors, and only one performance a day; it was a small theatre, whose audience never numbered more than ten. Buha was born and raised in Seoul, but had never known that such a theatre existed in this city. The audience was made up of blind people, or of students, mainly, who would be assigned to write school reports on the performance. The poet woman worked alone all day, selling tickets to visitors alone, arranging the library's documents alone and, once the performance was over, locking up alone. She seemed to enjoy this work. Now and then, while she worked, an inscrutable smile would appear on her face. But that only happened when she was alone. The poet woman stayed inside the theatre all day. Listening to the weather forecast on the radio was almost a hobby of hers, though not the ordinary forecast but the shipping forecast, for the weather out at sea.

At times Buha had trailed her – though the criminal connotations of such a word meant he hesitated to use it to describe his own actions. He didn't expect anything from her. The present situation, in which he simply looked at her, could not have suited him better. All he wanted was to watch her, for as long as possible, even if only from behind, with no other aim or ulterior motive.

One day the poet woman took the subway for some distance, all the way to the end of the line. There, she switched to a bus. The bus pierced the barren residential areas where the city's outskirts had been erected on haggard earth, passed through a vast suburban district dotted here and there with low apartment buildings and lonely petrol stations. The poet woman alighted at a secluded bus stop. The darkness lacked even a single point of light. No houses or other buildings could be seen, but that would have been due to the darkness only, not because they did not exist. It looked like a patch of reclaimed land, the kind that would boast only a small closed-down factory whose owner had gone bankrupt and then killed themselves, or a warehouse – deserted after sunset – where dubious business was conducted. There, the roads were almost empty, the sky black without a moon or stars. Sometimes cars with their headlights on sped along the road. There was absolutely no reason to stop in such a place. At the desolate roadside, which resembled a concrete desert, there was only the bus stop shelter. The empty lot behind the stop was strewn with rubbish: broken bricks, a car with its windscreen broken and its tyres gone, a destroyed cupboard and a sofa. A dog barked, its precise location unknown but close by. Not a pet raised at home, but a hefty animal. It barked threateningly, and others took up the call. There were countless dogs in the darkness. Invisible heavy chains clanked drearily as they tugged at invisible iron bars. The appearance of someone unknown, unfamiliar, alien sent a ripple of unrest through the animals' night.

The poet woman took a small road to the rear of the empty lot, then trudged on without looking back. Gradually her footsteps grew swifter. She headed straight to the heart of the darkness, which lacked even a single point of light, and where not even the road beneath her feet could be seen. Like a blind owl, she walked as one with the darkness, undisturbed by it. The sight called up in Buha simultaneous awe and fear. The barking of dogs drew closer. It occurred to Buha that pursuing the poet woman any further might result in needless terror and agitation, for her or else for himself. That was not what Buha wanted. He did not want the poet woman to turn around, having sensed a human presence. He didn't want her to see him. He didn't want her to know him. And so he stood, rooted to the spot. The woman's shadow was swiftly swallowed up into the abyss of darkness.

Buha was tired after returning home so late, but still he picked up the receiver and dialled freelancer Yeoni's number.

'Please, take me to another world,' he said.

'I invite you into the ecstasy of my dream. We're leaving now. Take my hand.' Yeoni's low voice stole soft as breath into Buha's ear, making the tiny hairs on his skin stand up.

'Where are we going?'

'We're looking for a place that has so far remained unknown.'

'Does such a place really exist?'

'Yes. Close your eyes and touch my skin.'

'Will we discover the unknown place?' Buha asked with his eyes closed.

'We seek three caves.' Yeoni's voice ran on without the slightest hesitation. 'The first cave is a private space that draws us in; because we ourselves once came out of it. Nectar of the poppy gushes warm from the secret stream inside the cave. The nectar is fragrant and sweet. The stream is our beginning and end. We're drawn inside it as swiftly as ants into an ant lion's pit . . . since the second is a cave of illusions and apparitions, it takes us to a very distant land.' Yeoni's voice grew lower. 'We are walking across the arid steppe, carrying a jar of liquor; at each step we take, the milky liquid lapping at the mouth of the jar spatters our feet. From the white liquid comes the scent of alcohol distilled from leaves. Our tongues are on fire. And so, though we raise the jar and try drinking the white alcohol inside it, our thirst is never quenched. In the distance a volcano explodes with a single, awful groan. Jets of grey ash and magma are propelled into the air. It is the moment nature and matter die simultaneously. Suspension of consciousness, and blackout. The moment the movement of pupils stops, when blood is arrested in veins. The moment all colours and sounds disappear and all identity and density are extinguished. But we desire only to drink the droplets of white alcohol inside the jar. Then, when the ash engulfs the sky, at that moment when gods and humans and dinosaurs meet death simultaneously, that is . . .'

With both eyes still closed, Buha opened his mouth as though to receive the final drop of white alcohol, but nothing landed on his dry lips and tongue.

'The third cave is the place of a cult,' Yeoni's voice continued like a slow wave. 'A dark place of severe secrecy. In the very heart of the secret is the most private, frightening and forbidden place of all. It is known as a place where women lusting after a bull or men who sleep with their daughters go. But according to a different rumour, the forbidden is nothing more than a human-induced hallucination. Taboo is an even more primal fantasy than religion. It is also said that the fearful awe evoked by the place was long ago reduced, paradoxically, to a means of increasing pleasure, rather than the fear that was its origin. Our sleep now flows into this third cave. We go forwards without looking back, our bodies given over to the cave's energy. We are beside ourselves. We are captivated. Something sucks hard at our flesh and souls. We are no longer ourselves. We are one with the secret outside us, one body. It is a stifling unease and a chest-tightening terror. But it is also an incomparable fascination and joy. Bewitched, we are compelled to approach ever closer to the taboo.'

Buha was asleep. Unable to move his limbs, to twitch a finger or even blink, yet in his sleep he was still able to hear freelancer Yeoni's whispering. From far away came the faint sound of a dog barking. Not a pet raised at home, but a hefty animal the size of a cow. It barked threateningly, and others took up the call. There were countless dogs in the darkness. Invisible heavy chains clanked drearily as they tugged at invisible iron bars. In his sleep, Buha thought of himself dreaming of a deep cave, and listening to Yeoni's undulating whispers.

'By now you will have become aware that the third cave corresponds to the third hole of the flesh and blood body that belongs to me. But the cave also belongs to you. It was only through you that it acquired its particular character. The body is a passageway – a channel, without which the two of us would not be able to exist in the way we do now, the way I know you and you know me. Without their mirror images, our original forms would not exist. The third cave is the third mirror. Love is the act of wandering in search of an unknown cave. Somewhere underground, deep, dark, echoing, amplified, frightening, bewitching, and utterly private, a secret for me, a single ship, a single concealed place.'

★

Buha planned to go the library to look for the poet woman's collection. But in the small provincial library the poet woman's name didn't appear in the catalogue. It seemed she hadn't written any poetry for a long time.

Maybe she changed her name, Buha thought.

Buha found the periodicals room, hoping at least to read the interview from twenty years before.

'Twenty years ago?' The librarian looked up at Buha with wide eyes. 'This library's not even been open four years. For anything dating that far back, you'd have to go to the municipal library.'

Buha took the bus and then the subway to the municipal library, where, after perusing all the newspapers from the past twenty-odd years – as he couldn't remember exactly when it was that he'd read the interview with the poet woman – Buha discovered one small article related to her. The article stated that the poet woman, aged forty-nine, had been found dead in the space between the ceiling and roof of her house in Huam-dong within a month of going missing. This was certainly news to Buha, and he found the whole thing somewhat suspicious. Still more suspicious was that the police had judged the poet woman's death to be suicide. Because, though it was a highly unusual place for someone to choose to kill themselves, there was no sign of forced entry and no wounds to the body. Further, a fatal tumour had been found in her chest, and the cause of death looked to be starvation. They said she had probably chosen the place to avoid being discovered after she died. The newspaper was called *24/7 Incidents*, a weekly whose hyperbolic, sensationalistic articles tended to lack credibility.

Since none of the other papers mentioned the incident, there was no way for Buha to know if he should take the article at face value, if the poet woman's name had been recorded incorrectly, or if it was a different person with the same name.

The other basis for doubt was a separate article in a different newspaper – more reputable than *24/7 Incidents* – published at about the same time that autumn. This other article was a report on an exhibition of amateur photographers in a Seoul theatre known as the 'Red Salon'; the name of the person who had given a poetry reading at the opening was that of the poet woman. According to those who had been at the Red Salon for the opening, the woman had been wearing a short dress embellished with silver foil reminiscent of mackerel scales, her hair was so long it reached the base of her spine, and her face, deeply wrinkled, was riddled with smallpox scars and unsightly splotches. 'It had only been a little over a year since we'd met, but her appearance had been shockingly transformed,' one witness said. A female poet of the same name and age as the poet woman Buha knew.

He spent the rest of the afternoon reading manhwa in old newspapers.

Several elderly retirees also sat quietly in the periodicals room, devouring old newspapers. Positioned apart like islands, they maintained their distance peacefully, staying out of each other's way. They had come to the library expressly to read newspapers from the past two decades. One, who looked to be over ninety, was transcribing a newspaper article into a notebook, letter by letter, in pencil.

When five o'clock approached, the librarian came over to let them know that the room was closing.

Buha wandered aimlessly along the street in front of the municipal library, then went into a snack bar crowded with teenage boys in school uniforms and ate a bowl of noodles with twigim.

Afterwards, Buha caught a bus outside the snack bar and the boys jostled their way on behind him, talking loudly until they all piled out at the same stop. Buha alighted with them; he hadn't intended to take the bus so far, but had become engrossed in their conversation. Apparently the students were on their way to an audio theatre, tasked with listening to a performance and then writing a report about it. Of course, a performance with no visual element was not especially appealing to a bunch of teenagers, but they were still expecting it to be better than an art installation or a Shostakovich recital. According to one, the fact that it was made up of words would at least make writing the report less tricky. Buha sat next to them, propping up his forehead with the heel of his hand, pretending to nod off.

Listening to the students' language, pungent words roughly and crudely pronounced, Buha recalled how he had been at their age: timid, introverted, easily embarrassed. The high school he'd attended had been utterly run-of-the-mill. Meaning it had been overrun with gangsters. One kid in Buha's class set up an on-demand department store, and pestered the others to buy shoes, cigarettes, comic books featuring naked women, etc. Now and then pupils did indeed put in orders for various items. He bragged that he could fulfil any request, even for a Japanese girlfriend.

The young entrepreneur had also been at the same middle school as Buha and was unfailingly friendly towards him, asking several times if there were something he could source for him, but Buha always declined the offer. Buha was so introverted that he had few friends, and attracted little notice from the teachers. Perhaps he was lucky, because the high school mafia generally left him alone. It was a strict school, but it wasn't the discipline or the gangs or the perennially unsatisfying sexual experiences that dealt a fatal blow to Buha's sensibility, but a girl student he encountered on the way home. She had been walking in front of him for a long time with an enormous stain of dark red menstrual blood on her light grey summer skirt.

The moment her figure entered his field of vision Buha seemed to freeze on the spot in shock and terror. Her measured pace meant Buha could neither overtake her nor slow down sufficiently to allow her to vanish into the distance. The girl walked in exactly the same direction as Buha. He was terrified that she would turn to look back for some reason, and that their gazes would collide. The girl's period stain was too large for Buha to avert his eyes or pretend he hadn't seen it. Even in his state of paralysis, Buha was aware that he absolutely did not want to see the girl's face. He didn't want to know her face. He didn't want to know her. To know that she had beautiful hair so black it was almost blue, beautiful long, delicate limbs, and a face severely pitted with smallpox scars. He didn't want her unique, particular face to fix in his mind. But that moment the founder of the on-demand department store and his minions – all kid gangsters – swept past Buha from behind on their bicycles. They cheered joyfully as they went by, as they always did when set free from school. Whistling enthusiastically and ringing their bells in unison. It sounded as though all the bells in the world were jangling at once. The wind from the passing bicycles whipped Buha's cheeks. It was the insane delight and speed of life. It seemed to him that he had ended up walking between two simultaneously existing worlds. As in fact he had.

'Oh, I'm sorry.'

Lost in thought, Buha had bumped into a cane, and now he bowed and apologised, flustered. But since the girl holding the cane was blind, these gestures would have gone unnoticed. The girl had been on the point of slipping inside the audio theatre. Its glass door was open, and the poet woman was preparing to sell tickets at a small table by the entrance. The afternoon sunlight heated the nape of her neck. The asphalt blazed. Buha moved out of the blind girl's way. When the girl turned, the skirt of her white hanbok twirled with her body, giving off the scent of strongly starched cotton. Immediately Buha felt his chest tighten with anxiety. But the girl's skirt was as clean as a baby. Unconscious of his own actions, Buha handed two thousand-won notes to the poet woman. She reached out and took his money without even glancing up. The male high school students bought tickets after Buha.

Having never been inside the audio theatre before, Buha passed slowly in front of the reading room, entered the auditorium and sat down next to the male students, who by then had overtaken him and stationed themselves on the sofas. The blind girl tapped the floor with her cane as she entered, seeming familiar with the layout. Only after Buha had sat down did he examine the programme, where the title of the day's performance was printed: *The Blind Owl*. The same performance was running all week. And, according to the programme, this would be the last performance ever held at the audio theatre.

One of the male students snickered to himself as he looked over at the blind girl. Then, as soon as his eyes locked with Buha's, he abruptly swallowed his laughter. He glared at Buha, as though he thought he was being admonished. The poet woman walked down the stairs to the small stage area, approached the audio equipment and inserted a CD into one of the machines.

'Today's performance is Sadeq Hedayat's *The Blind Owl*,' she announced.

Buha found himself listening very closely to her voice. He held himself rigid to catch the sound of each word, even holding his breath.

The poet woman left a brief pause after her first sentence, then continued:

'Hedayat was an Iranian writer, and *The Blind Owl* is his major work. The book is highly regarded, and is a pessimistic, atmospheric work filled with dreams, visions and agonies. In particular, the mysterious repeated statements enhance the sense of the surreal, the fantastical. Hedayat was born in

Tehran, studied in Belgium and France, worked as an ordinary bank clerk on his return to Iran, and later travelled for a year in India, which is where he wrote *The Blind Owl*. He was also a translator of Kafka, bringing *The Metamorphosis* into Persian for the first time. He had one failed suicide attempt, that we know of. He was twenty-four, studying in Paris. One day, on the way home from meeting friends in a cafe, he found an old bridge at a secluded spot over the Seine, and threw himself into the water. Unbeknown to him, a couple were making love in a boat beneath the bridge. The man jumped straight into the water and saved Hedayat from drowning (which he would have done otherwise, as he didn't know how to swim). Hedayat spent his career in near-obscurity, denied literary recognition in Iran apart from by those who cynically ridiculed his work. Not only that, the fact that the literary scene was intensely influenced by the West made his point of view an awkward one politically. He never married. In 1950, a close friend and doctor wrote an official diagnosis stating that Hedayat had an illness that was impossible to treat in Tehran. It was thanks to this that he was able to leave Iran. He went back to Paris and, there, in April 1951, ended his life by suicide . . .' The poet woman paused. 'OK, the play will begin now.'

The male students were busily transcribing the poet woman's words in the margins of their programmes. But they looked disappointed that she hadn't said more about the work itself. The poet woman wore a white blouse and a summer skirt that flopped like an old dishcloth. When she turned, the movement of her skirt exposed skinny calves corded with stringy muscle, pathetically small feet, and shoes that gleamed like new but looked like cast-offs. Her hair was tied back in a low ponytail. She was the model of an unpretentious, ordinary young woman dressed in old-fashioned clothes. In Buha's eyes, the poet woman seemed to have little interest in external appearance or standards of beauty. He remembered her as always dressing the same. As though perhaps she had no other clothes.

The poet woman flicked on the audio switch. Some brief introductory music played, and then the protagonist's monologue began.

'In life there are wounds that, like leprosy, slowly eat away at the soul, in solitude . . .'

It was the voice of the poet woman, which he had heard for the first time that same day. Yet it was also a voice he knew.

They might have known each other for far longer than Buha had thought. The poet woman's voice was the third cave they were searching for. Because, when the poet woman opened her mouth on the television screen from which no sound came, freelancer Yeoni's voice spoke the following words from the other end of the telephone line:

Do not – go – far away – even – for just – one – day
– because
Because – a day – is long – and
I – will wait – for you.

Buha was standing outside the glass door of the audio theatre. In that narrow alley there were locals out for an evening stroll, people on their way home from work, a blue car driven by a middle-aged woman, and a man and woman holding hands, either an ordinary couple or else primary school classmates meeting again after four decades had passed. They all moved forwards at a fixed pace until, as though something had suddenly occurred to them, they paused and looked up at a street sign, at the display window of a small store, at pedestrians passing along the street, or at the sky. A man carrying a kitten in a cage bumped into Buha. The man stammered an apology, concealing his mouth with the sleeve of the heavy coat he wore despite the muggy weather, and then hurried away like a thief. Gazing after him, Buha's immediate thought was that he was a pickpocket who had made off with his wallet. After all, this was the typical modus operandi of a pickpocket: bumping into someone, then hastily disappearing. Buha felt a surge of irritation, and reached into his pocket for his wallet. It wasn't there. But then he recalled that he had come out with only a few notes that day, leaving his wallet at home. He didn't like the bulge it made in his pocket.

The man and woman who looked like an ordinary couple holding hands, or else primary school classmates meeting again after four decades, stopped walking. The woman looked up, and the face framed by her long, excessively black hair bore conspicuous pockmarks on its dark skin. The man gestured towards the audio theatre with his dry, calloused hand. Gazing up at the man with an expression that went beyond mournful love, the woman with the pockmarked face said: 'Are you really going to leave me like you wrote in that letter?' At that, the woman's skirt fluttered like an old dishcloth in the still air, exposing skinny calves corded with stringy muscle, pathetically small feet, and shoes that gleamed like new yet looked like cast-offs.

The sight sent an unbearable pain shooting through Buha's head. The pain was so extreme that a scream burst from him. A metal bell rang crazily in his ears. He was rooted to the spot. It felt as if someone were hammering a nail into the crown of his head. With each blow, all Buha could do was grip his head desperately. Stumbling forwards, flailing, directionless.

Once the pain had eased somewhat, Buha looked up, dizzy. The poet woman's face was right there – in front of his eyes – so close he could see his dishevelled figure distinctly reflected in her round pupils. Those pupils were large, fully dilated, the outermost petals of an unfurled flower, wholly seized by some kind of emotion, given over to it, yet unmoving. Before he knew what he was doing, Buha's hands were covering her face. Her unmoving face was right there beneath his palms. A face that said: I am emotion. But in reality, his outstretched palms, faintly sticky with the heat, were touching not her face but the glass door. The theatre door was closed, and the poet woman was on the other side. She slowly raised both hands as though in response and brought them to the place where Buha's hands were. Their hands overlapped without touching. Hearts throbbed quiet and fast. Blood formed a frightening whirlpool, beating on the walls of their veins. Still with that space between them, they became one.

We are nothing: the poet woman's moving lips seemed to pronounce these words. Though the glass door was thick enough to be sound-proof, Buha felt sure in that moment that this was what she was saying to him: We are nothing. Now, we are nothing. We have gone back to being nothing.

'For such a long time we . . . we've known each other so long . . . so intimately; you know we have!' Buha blurted this out in spite of himself, gripped by an intense emotion. 'The light in your eyes, your voice, everything about you is so close and intimate!'

At that, the poet woman spoke what seemed to be the following sentence, moving her lips exaggeratedly: 'That's over now, I'm telling you it's over.'

'For God's sake, it can't end like this! Don't do this! Please, open the door!'

No, I can't open the door. The poet woman shook her head.

'Why can't you?'

Because I'll die if I do.

'Die? What nonsense! You're not going to die! You're going to grow old with me, you'll live a long, long time! You're not going to die! I'm telling you, you're not!' Buha waved his arms wildly, his voice low but intense. He became aware that two security guards who had been watching him were now approaching. The guards grabbed his arms, but their reprimands were not audible to Buha. 'I'm not mad, I'm not drunk, I haven't done anything to her; we've known each other for a long time, we've been . . . gazing at each other for a long time, we're going to carry on for a long time, too.'

The guards paid no mind to his mutterings. They dismissed him as mad. Or simply drunk. Once the lights changed, the blue car driven by a middle-aged woman roared away. Wide-eyed and stiff as a statue, the poet woman watched Buha from the far side of the glass door. His dishevelled figure was reflected in her large, unmoving pupils. Buha's form was being sucked into the poet woman's eyes. With neither motion nor sound, like particles of sand being drawn body and soul through the narrow opening in an hourglass. That strangely gaunt face, where the eye sockets were sunken like caves, the lips were dry, and the whites of the eyes were distinctly webbed with red capillaries.

3

It was around midday when they opened their eyes. Through the curtainless window the midday heat thrust itself into the narrow room. They were dazzled, like lidless eyeballs.

It wasn't because they were sufficiently rested that they'd woken, nor because the day was too bright. It was only because it was so hot. Unendurably so. The room itself was blazing. Still half asleep, they took beer and cucumber from the fridge. The fridge seemed almost magical; each time the door opened there was beer and cucumber inside.

The other thing that had woken them was Ayami's phone ringing under the pillow. Still holding the cucumber, Ayami answered the phone with her free hand.

She had a short conversation made up of brief, one-word answers.

'Who on earth would call at a time like this?' the man grumbled after she was done.

'It was the broadcasting company,' Ayami said. 'And it's midday, so not at all an inappropriate time for a phone call.'

'I meant, when it's so insanely hot,' the man muttered to himself, clutching a can of beer. 'Have we been asleep for that long? How is it midday already?'

The tone of his voice was recognisably peevish. He looked around the cramped room. On the table by the bed was a blue medicine bottle, ingredients unknown, and on the shelf was a large boxy yellow radio, the kind found in antique shops or flea markets. His eye was caught by the only book on the shelf: *The Blind Owl*, by a writer he hadn't heard of. With the bed and other furniture, there was barely enough space for one person to turn around without knocking into something. The only window opened onto a dirty wall, preventing anything resembling fresh air from circulating, and seeming instead to stop the invading sunlight and heat from escaping. On the narrow windowsill stood a candle, half melted by the sunlight into a crooked slump, and by the medicine bottle on the table were a pencil and paper, as if someone had been in the middle of writing a letter.

The man rolled onto his side and started muttering again.

'It's so muggy, it's worse than a wet quilt . . . I've hardly slept. . . I'll have to get into a tub of cold water if I want to sleep. . . where's the bathroom?'

'There isn't one.' Ayami answered with her eyes closed, crunching on cold cucumber. Like her, the man had been half asleep, but this response made his eyes snap open.

'What? Then, where's the shower?'

'There's a tap and a bucket in the kitchen; you can wash yourself there.' Ayami spoke slowly, calmly, matter-of-fact.

'What?' the man exclaimed, clearly put out. 'A tap?'

Heaving himself up, he went to investigate the adjoining kitchen, discovered the dripping tap, and shook his head.

He returned to the room and flung himself back down onto the bed. 'A tap? I've flown twelve hours from the other side of the world and I can't even have a cold shower, and have to sweat like a pig instead.'

Still grumbling to himself, the man picked up his can of beer and drained it. Then closed his eyes. Exhausted, he fell straight back asleep. A few hours later he opened his eyes again. By now – you – will have become aware – that – the third – cave – corresponds to – the third – hole – of the flesh – and blood – body – that belongs – to me – But – the cave – also – belongs – to you – It was only – through you – that – it – acquired – its – particular – character – What – are – we? – if – there – was no – communication – no – exchange – through the body . . . Today's. Temperature. Forty. Degrees. Celsius. No wind. No cloud. Danger. Of burning. Forty. Degrees. Absence. Of wind. Absence. Of cloud. Daytime. City. Mirage. Scheduled. To appear. Absence. Of wind. Absence. Of cloud. Absence. Of colour. In the sky.

'What's that?' the man asked, lying flat on his back.

'The radio,' Ayami replied, perching on the edge of the bed as she peeled off her sweat-soaked blouse.

'Why would you put the radio on?' There was suppressed anger in the man's voice.

'It came on by itself.'

'Then switch it off.'

'I can't. That's impossible.'

'Why is it impossible?'

'The radio . . . the switch is broken, you see? So it comes on automatically, then switches itself off again.'

'Can you pull out the plug?'

'No, that's impossible.'

'Why is it impossible?'

'I . . . I'm afraid of electrical noise. It's frightening, like the sound of gas hissing, or knives, or lightning.'

All traces of sleep had left the man's face.

'Yeoni,' he said slowly, still lying flat on his back, 'it's like you're deliberately trying to make me angry.'

'No, I'm not. See, now the radio's stopped. Once you become used to it, it won't bother you. And I'm not Yeoni.'

'You're not Yeoni? Then who are you?' The man looked shocked. 'The editor said, "Yeoni will come and meet you when you arrive at Incheon." So last night, no, this morning, when we met, I naturally assumed you were Yeoni.'

'I thought you knew what Yeoni looks like. That you once sat next to each other on a train in Europe. Is that not true?'

'That wasn't me, it was my editor who sat next to a woman called Yeoni on a train and ended up travelling with her. He asked her to help me with my work.' The man sighed. 'So, no, of course I've never set eyes on this woman; I wasn't even aware of her existence until the editor told me about her. I don't know anything about her other than her name. Anyway, whoever Yeoni is, what I do know is that if I'm not able to produce a manuscript this time, my editor will kill me.'

'Yeoni asked me the same thing your editor asked her. To help you with your poetry. But nothing concrete about how exactly I could help a poet's writing.'

'I'm no poet,' the man said brusquely. 'Not that the label offends me, exactly, it's just so over the top. Some flowery, romantic notion of what I do.'

'Then who are you?'

'I'm called Wolfi.'

'If you're not a poet who's come to Korea to write, what are you here for?'

'I'm here to write, that's true. But not poetry.'

'Then what kind of writing?'

'I write detective fiction.'

'I'm sorry. Yeoni said you were a poet.'

'There's no need to be sorry. But it does make me wonder how this Yeoni described me.'

'A poet is coming.'

'What?'

'She just said, "A poet is coming."'

They turned their heads and looked straight at each other.

The detective novelist had a round, plump face, a long, slightly stooped back, and long arms. The hair plastered to his forehead was dark brown and his shirt, now dark with sweat, was light brown when dry. When the afternoon sun shone most brightly into this house, the detective writer's eyes beneath his thick brown brows were such a pale hazel that they became translucent. In the dazzling afternoon sun, the lashes surrounding his eyes, and each strand of hair on his arms and the backs of his hands, were so saturated by the light they became almost colourless.

His was a face that could look thirty-five or forty-five, depending on circumstances, a type of face Ayami had never seen so close up.

'But, anyway, it must be the middle of today now. Unless we've slept a whole day through, and it's actually tomorrow?'

'It's the middle of today,' Ayami confirmed, 'not the middle of tomorrow.' Her voice betrayed no hint of humour. 'But to be precise, it's quite a bit past the middle. Six in the evening, in fact.'

'What? Wasn't it noon just a little while ago?'

'It was a little before six.'

'I must have fallen asleep. Though it's a mystery how a person can sleep in a room as hot as this.'

'I don't know if it'll comfort you to know, but . . . it's hotter outside.'

'How do you know?'

'I went out for a bit.'

'Ever since I landed at the airport last night, no, early this morning, it's been like one long nightmare,' Wolfi sighed. 'It feels as though . . . as though I'd wanted to take a plane to Helsinki, but got the transfer gate confused, and ended up taking a ridiculous plane to a ridiculous country, flying a ridiculously long time only to arrive at the wrong destination. A country where I can't understand a word of the language, where there's no tourist information, and where I don't know a single person, not even a name.'

'Even so, someone did meet you at the airport.'

'But it wasn't the person I was expecting – Yeoni of Helsinki – but some other ridiculous woman. So now I have the same feeling again, that I got on the wrong plane to the wrong destination. I can't even be sure where "here" is any more. You could tell me we're in Beijing or Taipei, and I'd just have to take your word for it. But right now I have the feeling that we're in Seoul, is that correct?'

'Correct,' Ayami replied.

'I was already having trouble sleeping before flying out so, last night, no, early this morning, I was utterly exhausted. And what do I find when I land but that the so-called international airport is in the middle of a blackout. For the first time ever, or so they tell me. Dark, pitch-black, blurred, all objects shrouded in shadow, a blind low-ceilinged space. The immigration line stretched on forever; worst of all was the stifling air, like hot fog sticking to my skin, like a swarm of invisible leeches, unbearable. I had to queue for an hour before I reached the immigration desk. The lights and air conditioning still hadn't come back on. I was completely exhausted. That's why last night, no, early this morning, I wasn't able to muster the strength to ask you anything. I think I passed out as soon as we got into the taxi. And then of course I had to drag a heavy suitcase all the way up the hill. The sun wasn't even fully up but it was already so hot, and the air was muggy as a sauna, so I literally became a ball of sweat. But I was so tired I didn't even have the energy to change out of my clothes or wash my face, just collapsed onto the bed and fell asleep, you know. Of course, I didn't come here to soak in a hotel tub with a sea view, wake up to a continental breakfast and spend the day working on a marble balcony, sipping a Singapore Sling. I'm not one of those aristocratic writers. My editor knows that better than anyone. I'm here because my female protagonist dies. My female protagonist whose name and identity I still don't know, that is. Where does she come from? Who is she? I have her living somewhere in Asia. More specifically, in some city in the Far East that I'm not familiar with, in the house of a woman called Yeoni. She's an unlucky woman. Not Yeoni, but my female protagonist. Or maybe Yeoni is my "she", my female protagonist? In any case, Yeoni has a man but no money. Having said that, all money is the same, while every man is different. So the issue would be the kind of man she has. But when it comes to luck, do I really have it any better? I wanted to write by following her footsteps. That's why I've flown all the way over here. But I couldn't have imagined that I'd end up sweating to death in a shabby concrete shack with no bathroom, halfway up a mountain in Seoul. I doubt there's even room for a corpse in this house. If you absolutely needed to hide a dead body in here, you'd probably have to cram it between the ceiling and the roof. I'll have to look and see whether it would be possible. But it's just occurred to me that I might have ended up in this ridiculous place because I've been kidnapped. Kidnapped by an unknown woman I mistook for Yeoni.'

'Don't speak so quickly. Don't say so many things all at once, and don't use too much irony. Otherwise I won't understand a word.'

'It doesn't really matter, it's not especially important for either of us. But if you're not Yeoni, who on earth are you? No, there's no need to explain, just tell me your name, so I know what to call you. What's your name?'

'Ayami.'

'Where on earth did you go out to in this heat, Ayami?'

'To the broadcasting studios.'

'You work there?'

'No. I went for something else.'

Ayami got up, walked to the kitchen, turned on the tap, filled a bucket with water and began to wash her body. For a while there was the sound of water splashing onto the cement floor, then it stopped. When she returned to the room Wolfi, now sitting up, took a leaflet out of his pocket and showed it to her.

'This strange thing was in my pocket,' he said. 'I think I had my pocket picked at the airport. I escaped out of the pitch-black customs area, and in the darkness everybody merged with their bags and suitcases, fusing together like shadows worn thin; they looked like ghosts, passing through a station to the other world. Carrying backpacks and pushing trolleys, as though the weight and bulk of their luggage were a final, definitive record of who they had been in life, like a funeral guestbook. A man shoved past me. At first I assumed he was a lunatic who had lost his head in the heat, because he wore a heavy coat despite the weather, and also covered his mouth with one long, wide sleeve. It seemed something like a cage was concealed inside his sleeve, but I couldn't see well enough to be sure – as I've already said, there was a blackout, so the only point of illumination was the very faint lighting for the emergency exit. I thought, you know, maybe it's a stroke of luck that I didn't have my bank card with me. I'd done well to put my wallet in my backpack rather than a jacket pocket. Careful, Wolfi, this is a foreign country. Not just any foreign country, but one you've never visited and whose language is utterly unknown to you. I tried to find a policeman to point out the man in the coat, but so little was visible in the blackout. It would have been pointless anyway. Any policeman would have used the blackout as an excuse for a nap. Where would I have found one? Would they have understood English?'

'Don't speak so quickly. Don't say so many things all at once, and don't use too much irony. Otherwise I won't understand a word.'

'Damn it, this is crazy. I thought that guy must have shoved past me to pick my pocket!'

'And did he? What did he steal?'

'Well, it seems he wasn't a pickpocket after all. At least, if he was, he didn't take anything. The opposite: he put something in. When I reached into my pocket just now I found this strange leaflet . . . it looks like an ad for an exhibition!'

'You're right,' Ayami said, examining the paper, 'this is an ad for a photography exhibition. *Where do we come from? What are we? Where are we going?*'

'What are you talking about?'

'It's the title of the exhibition. *Where do we come from? What are we? Where are we going?*'

'You really do have a strange way of publicising exhibitions here,' Wolfi said, his voice betraying no hint of sarcasm. 'Is it a Korean photographer?'

'The photographs are taken by poets, not professional photographers.'

'Poets!'

'We can go if you're interested, it's on in a theatre not far from here. Plus, today's the opening, so it'll run until late.'

'Sure. I need to get an idea of what the downtown area looks like.'

'This morning at the airport . . .' Ayami spoke slowly, 'I was startled to see the world vanish in front of my eyes. The customs area with its glaring lighting, the exit doors, you yourself, soon to appear from behind them – it was all just extinguished, no bang, no crack. As though my eyes had disappeared, rather than the objects themselves. I raised my hand unconsciously and groped the air in front of me. But when I blinked there were forms in the darkness. Forms with no substance . . . like ghosts flying slowly, too late. Souls left behind on earth even after the death of matter.'

'But what I still don't understand is how we were able to make each other out in the dark.'

'After you came through the gate, you walked straight towards me.'

'That was complete coincidence. I was just walking blindly forwards.'

'And like someone greeting me, like someone standing in the shadow of a statue in the centre of a public square, you raised your hand. Hesitated only for a moment, then slowly waved at me.'

'I'm telling you, Ayami, that was all coincidence. I was only trying to feel my way through the darkness; I couldn't see in front of me, and it was making me feel suffocated.'

'So I knew it was you.'

★

Ayami sat on the windowsill next to the crooked candle and dried her hair. The exhibition leaflet was on her knee. The scent of steaming rice rose from the pot in the kitchen. Into the cramped single room lacking both air con and fan, hot air heavier than a sodden quilt was pressing itself through the window like lumps of warm flesh.

Wolfi had been watching Ayami in silence. 'What do you do?' he asked now.

'I'm an actor. Though I don't have any work right at the moment.'

'Ah, so that's why someone called from the broadcasting agency,' Wolfi muttered to himself. 'Have you appeared in films? Or on stage?'

'I've acted in front of a camera only once, in a performance film by a very young director. It was a four-minute film. With no script.'

'A performance film?'

'We just had to keep talking, improvise. We met at a Burger King downtown. It was around midnight. But there were three specific words we had to use in our conversation.'

'Which ones?'

'Nappy, Greece and secret.'

'Be quiet, I just got a call from Greece, it's a secret so no one must listen in, but what's that? Oh dear, there's a nappy on the floor; something like that?'

'That's right.'

'What character did you play? If it had characters, that is.'

'I was a blind girl. I went into the Burger King wearing coarse cotton clothes and hemp sandals, holding a white cane, I deliberately bumped into an actor in a brown suit and began a conversation with him.'

'How exciting.'

'We each talked about an aunt. A rich aunt.'

'I've got an aunt like that. She bought a big house with three grand pianos and a swimming pool. A prickly, intimidating character. But she died a long time ago. In a car accident.'

'A car accident; do you mean a bus?'

'No. She was pinned beneath a car at the zebra crossing. Her kidneys were so mangled she couldn't urinate, and suffered like that for almost two months before she died.'

'Strange,' Ayami said, gazing earnestly at Wolfi's face.

'There's nothing strange about my aunt dying; the car crushed her stomach.'

'Not that – it's strange that I'm not able to read your lips.'

'You can lip-read?'

'Yes. Most of the time. I'm able to understand most of what you say, but being unable to read lips is unfamiliar. An unfamiliar sensation.'

They took more beer and cucumber from the fridge. It seemed almost magical: every time the door opened there was beer and cucumber inside.

'Around this time each year I dream of clutching an enormous parrot to my chest and crawling into a nonexistent bathtub brimming with cold water,' Ayami said. 'Digging its claws into my chest, the parrot shrieks, a loud and drawn-out shriek. And my emotions expand further than at any other time, extending over a vast territory.'

Though it hadn't been five minutes since Wolfi had bathed, already he felt the hot air clinging to his pores again, creating a slick sheen on his skin.

Wolfi got out his laptop, raised both index fingers like a pair of chopsticks and hammered out the following sentences: 'There was a dead woman's body in the ceiling, but this was still unknown. Where do we come from? What are we? Where are we going?'

'What are you mumbling?' Ayami called from the kitchen. 'Have you started writing?'

'I'm just making a note of first impressions,' Wolfi responded, continuing to tap away. 'Don't mind me.'

'I've only got plain rice, is that OK?'

Wolfi continued to type without answering; it was his habit to mutter the words as he typed them: 'Humid afternoon with the parrot's claws piercing my chest. Outside the window comes a cry both sorrowful and transcendent.'

After setting the food out on the desk-cum-dining table, Ayami removed a knee-length white cotton hanbok from the small wardrobe in a corner of the room, put it on, and secured her hair in a low ponytail. The hanbok material rustled when she moved, giving off the strong scent of starch.

'Is that some kind of special costume?' Wolfi asked.

'It's what I wore for the performance film.'

'Are you going out like that?'

'I don't have anything else. My other clothes are soaked with sweat.'

They sat at the table to eat. The side dishes were cucumber kimchi and cucumber salad. Thirst and the heat sent

Wolfi to the fridge for another beer. Despite being hungry, he ate very little of the unfamiliar food, including the steaming rice – it was too hot for him – but Ayami polished off one bowl and scooped herself another. Wolfi watched her with curiosity as he drank his beer.

Later that evening they went out, into air that was still blazing hot though the sun was low in the sky.

'Last night, no, this morning,' Wolfi said, 'tossing and turning in the cruel heat, you talked in your sleep; I couldn't understand what you were saying, of course, but were you having some kind of dream?'

'I dreamed I was a woman who sells alcohol,' Ayami answered calmly, looking ahead as they walked down the hill.

'A woman who sells alcohol?' Wolfi repeated, somewhat baffled. 'You mean a woman who works at a bar?'

'No. I mean Maria, who sells alcohol in the northern desert. Who fills a jar with home-brewed white liquor and stands by the roadside in the middle of the bleak, empty desert, selling the drink to thirsty truck drivers. One cup for ten cents.'

'So, did you sell a lot?'

'No.' Ayami shook her head. 'Just walked and walked all day. Though the dream would have lasted no more than a few minutes, a day in that world stretched on and on. That day was like for ever, like when people say "for ever and a day". I walked the arid wilderness carrying the heavy jar; each time I took a step the milky fluid lapping at the mouth of the jar spattered my feet. That white fluid gave off the scent of alcohol distilled from leaves. My tongue is on fire. I raise the jar and drink, but my thirst is never quenched.'

They took a bus and arrived at the exhibition space. Until recently – in fact, until the previous day – the small space had been South Korea's only audio theatre. They looked around for where to buy tickets before noticing a sign saying: 'This exhibition is free'. Inside, the ground-floor theatre was made up of a long, narrow lobby, one small auditorium, and an even smaller library. The door to the library was closed, and looking through the glass wall told them there was no one inside. The photographs were displayed in the auditorium, from which the sound equipment had been cleared away. Just as they were going inside, several male high school students were emerging. The students hurtled out into the lobby, yelling and shoving as they went. Ayami looked around, expecting to see a teacher in charge, but there was no one.

In the past, people were vaguely fearful of photographs, believing the camera's exact reproduction of their own image would steal their souls. Not only did these images survive for much longer than their subjects, they were also endowed with an aura of magic the subjects lacked. A superstition, but one whose traces can still be felt today. People sense that the photograph captures an uncanny moment in the interstices of reality, enhancing reality's eeriness, the root of which is unknown, and fixing that moment in place like a death mask. Photography differs from the art of painting in that capturing or exposing such a moment happens neither at the will of the photographer nor the one who is photographed. What is photographed is a ghost moment, clothed in matter. Photography is the dream of comprehensive meaning. Each object has parts of itself that are invisible. This territory, which neither the photographer nor the subject can govern, constitutes the secret kept by the object. Unrelated to the intention of either photographer or subject, within the magic of photography dwells a still, quiet shock. Try to imagine our house one day when we ourselves are no more. Somewhere in that house is the ghost of us, which will pass alone in front of a blind mirror, revealing our own blurred image.

Like these photographs, Wolfi thought.

He was standing in front of two images titled, respectively, *Honeymoon I* and *Honeymoon II*. *Honeymoon I* was a photograph of a woman. The woman stands in front of a building bearing a prominent relief. The relief consists of a row of abstract faces, resembling a painting by Paul Klee. On the building's ground floor is a display window of what looks like a high-end boutique; the relief covers the rest of the building's facade from the first floor upwards. It is a hot summer day, and a location popular with honeymooners; the woman is wearing a roughly starched white cotton dress, with no detailing or decoration. Her thick black hair is secured in a low ponytail, and rough hemp sandals poke out from beneath the hem of her skirt. She is gazing at the camera, her body facing forwards, defenceless. But as the camera had focused on a section of the facade, the woman's face is blurred. The large photograph is taken up mainly by the dark brown faces of the relief. Peculiar, symmetrical shamanistic faces recalling squid or monkey masks, each with individual expressions. The woman's reflection can be seen in the window of the boutique. Her hands are empty and slightly raised. The boutique window functions as a mirror, the passing cars and people walking by also reflected in its darkened surface, albeit indistinctly. They are all fixed in place, the limbs of the passers-by arrested mid-air, like the arms and legs of broken dolls.

Honeymoon II is of a swimming pool in a garden. It has an air of early morning, not long after sunrise, with cypress trees damp with dew in the weak light. At the bottom of the pool is a large water-filtering device resembling a narrow, cylindrical loofah, and a long hose leads out of the water. Thousand-legged centipedes, spiders and young snakes float on the surface with the unidentified dregs of black night. At the edge of the photo part of a sandstone villa is visible. In a room on the ground floor a blind woman is beating a quilt out of the window. She is the only person in the photograph. But there are wet footprints by the side of the pool. The footprints lead over the grass and disappear into the villa.

Where are they? Wolfi wondered. The newly wed couple are absent. The woman in *Honeymoon I* is alone, probably the man took the photograph, yet his reflection cannot be seen in the display window. And *Honeymoon II* has only one set of footprints.

Whatever the intention or aim of the photographer, Wolfi thought, every photograph is a unique proof of identity, firmly declaring that human beings are ghosts.

The exhibition space was a little like an amphitheatre, consisting of narrow flights of stairs divided by sofas. Visitors were able to peruse the works one by one while passing up and down the stairs. After the high school students had rushed out the only visitors were Ayami, Wolfi and an old man. Ayami was sitting on the second stair from the top, gazing at one of the photographs.

The old man came and stood next to Ayami, though he seemed oblivious to her presence. He was a shrunken figure, somewhat shorter even than she was, and so old it was extremely difficult to estimate his age. True, the space was air conditioned, but this was still the midsummer heatwave, so it was shocking to see him wearing a wide-sleeved grey-wool coat. It was a threadbare thing, its seams stretched, and had been patched in various places. With his thin, faded grey hair, his stooped back, his slack, lifeless neck, and tired eyes behind gleaming spectacles, he was like a rheumy old goat facing the butcher's axe. Those milky eyes were the oldest of his body's constituent parts. Hesitating, as though they still did not believe in their own ability to perceive the world, those eyes blinked ceaselessly and irregularly. At each spasmodic movement, the eyeballs themselves aged yet more rapidly.

The old man sat down next to Ayami. Together they gazed at the photograph.

'Do you like it?' the old man bleated with a goat's thin, quavering voice.

'It's very original,' Ayami answered. 'I wouldn't have thought a mangled bus could be the subject of a work of art.'

'Most people overlook the bus, but you spotted it right away!' A satisfied smile twitched the corners of his mouth.

'The title is *White Bus*,' Ayami said, with a tone of one stating the obvious.

'But people tend to focus on the highway, the square in front of the station, the statue of the general up there on his plinth, the density of the darkness, things like that. After all, the bus is only small, inconspicuous, hidden in the corner. They assume the photograph simply depicts an ordinary night scene in the city. Also, in the photograph the bus is no longer white.'

White Bus showed the deserted station square in the dead of night. The statue on its high plinth cast a long black shadow over the square. The statue had one arm half-raised, like a tour guide beginning an explanation to an invisible group. This was the heart of the city and yet all the lights were off, even the arcade of shops at the edge of the square was shrouded in darkness, and there were no vehicle head-lights. Next to the weighty mass of the pitch-black station, an elevated highway bisected the air. Beyond the highway were the contours of tall buildings, crowded together so that their bodies overlapped; stone slabs marking a giant's grave, and the giant was the city.

'Maybe you were too young to remember, but—' the old man exploded into a hacking cough, then carried on speaking, using his coat sleeve to wipe away drops of yellow saliva that had trickled from the corners of his mouth. 'That night, there was a city-wide blackout. All electric light was forbidden after midnight, and there was a curfew on almost all vehicles. There'd been a rumour that enemy planes might attack the city. A chaotic, stubborn rumour. But a rumour that came from the government.'

'Was this during the war?' Ayami asked.

'No. True, my generation experienced the Korean War first-hand, but . . . this photograph was taken two decades ago, so there was no war on, at least not that was known to us.'

The old man coughed again, so harshly it seemed his throat might burst. Then, pointing to a corner of the photograph, he carried on speaking in a voice so thin and metallic it was as if his larynx had been stuffed with wool. 'Here, this is where the bus fell.'

In the far background, a tiny bus could be seen upside down, its upper half completely crushed, beneath the elevated highway, the crash barrier torn apart. But as the bus had landed in the deep shadow, and because it was extremely distant from the camera and only took up an extremely small part of the photograph, at the extreme outer edge of the image, it wasn't instantly apparent that the photograph was also a photograph of the aftermath of a bus crash.

'The driver must not have heard about the blackout,' the old man continued. He was unflagging, though to look at him you would have thought speech came only with great effort. 'It wasn't an ordinary city bus, it had been privately hired. Strangely enough, that day the driver was alone, driving in circles but without any passengers. They said someone had asked him to do that all night around the downtown area . . . but that's only hearsay. During the day he lectured in aesthetics at a university, and at night he drove a bus. It must have been hard for him to stay awake – with two jobs leaving barely any time for sleep. Looking out on a road with no lights or other vehicles must have produced an odd, unfamiliar feeling in his exhausted brain. Maybe he was the only one who actually saw enemy fighter planes circling soundlessly in the black night sky, while the rest of us held our breath inside our homes and made sure the curtains were fully closed. He must have seen the blood-red searchlights of the planes and thought: A war is starting, the slaughter is beginning, watery blood is pooling on all the roofs. Or maybe he wouldn't have made the connection with war at all, and mistaken the searchlights for the arrival of a mythic dawn. But this is all just speculation.'

Ayami peered into the old man's small, reddened eyes, which festered behind his glasses as though they had already begun to rot. Dim grey specks crawled like insects towards his pupils.

'If that's true, then . . . how did you take this photograph?'

'I'm a poet. An unknown poet, of course.' The old man shrugged. 'The night of the blackout, a few journalists were given permission to film. Kind of like war correspondents. Though war hadn't broken out. Anyway, though I'm not a photographer, at the time I just happened to have been published in a newspaper, in a series called "My Favourite Poem", so the newspaper gave me the opportunity to take photographs that night. Photography has been my hobby ever since I was a child, you see. So when I published new books of poetry I would sometimes include a few of my photographs as well.'

'What happened to the bus driver?'

'He'd stopped breathing by the time the ambulance arrived.' The old man hacked up one more raucous cough, his whole body jerking violently. 'I'm sorry. When you're old the mucous membrane in your throat is ruined, and you find yourself coughing all the time.' He looked apologetically at Ayami. 'But, luckily enough, thanks to the support of the foundation I have my own photography exhibition, so . . . it's turned out pretty well. Without support, it's difficult to imagine an unknown poet like me, not to mention one so old, being offered an exhibition like this. Only yesterday this place was still an audio theatre. A theatre affiliated with the foundation. Then yesterday the theatre closed for good, and today a photography exhibition—'

'Then it's real?' Ayami cut the old man off.

'What do you mean?'

'The foundation. It really does exist?'

'Of course it does. Didn't I just tell you? They're the ones who made this whole thing possible.' The old man produced a small book from his pocket. 'I'd like to give you this book of mine as a memento,' he said, sounding somewhat bashful.

'A book that you wrote?'

'That's right.'

Ayami read the book's title out loud, but very quietly: '*Where do we come from? What are we? Where are we going?*'

'In fact, the exhibition's title is taken from the name of this collection,' the old man said, even more shyly, but as though something were compelling him to speak.

Ayami straightened her neck and looked at the old man.

'Then he's real?'

'What do you mean?'

'The poet Kim Cheol-sseok. He really does exist?'

'Of course. I am he. This person sitting here talking with you.' The old man muttered, through his wrinkled lips. 'You'd know this if you read the exhibition leaflet, but all three photographs are mine. *White Bus, Honeymoon I*, and *Honeymoon II*. Though it's been twenty years since I took them. Back then, I couldn't have imagined I'd outlast the things I was taking pictures of.' And the old poet laughed for a long time, bleating like a goat.

By the time Wolfi and Ayami stepped outside again the streets were buried in darkness. As soon as the lights changed to green at the four-way pedestrian crossing, a huge crowd rushed towards them. And they rushed towards the crowd.

'They're shadow soldiers,' Ayami whispered into Wolfi's ear. 'Hold on to my arm. This city's hidden name is "secret". People lose one another before they know it. Everything disappears as quickly as it's put up. The same is true of memories. It can happen that you take ten steps out of your door then turn and look back, and the house you just left isn't there any more. And then you'll never find it again. It can happen with people, too. This city's hidden name is "secret". So, hold on to my arm. You don't even have a phone, so if we're separated we have no way of contacting each other.'

'Is that right?' Having been unable to understand Ayami's words fully, Wolfi was somewhat perplexed, but lightly grasped her burning hot arm in its wrapping of rough cloth. 'OK, I believe you. Everyone here has the same colour hair. Your hair is black just like everyone else's, so if you were swept into the crowd it would be impossible for me to find you.' The asphalt had stored the heat of the daytime, and when they lowered their heads it scorched their faces in a sudden rush, like lava. Bumping and jostling against those coming in the opposite direction, they struggled across the road.

They sat on a bench at the foot of the statue in the square and shared out cola and ice between two paper cups whose wax coating had grown tacky in the heat. The cola became lukewarm as the ice rapidly melted. They stayed there even after the sun had fully set, because Wolfi had taken his laptop out of his backpack and begun to write. There was rubbish scattered around the bench: packaging from a Burger King meal, a dirty quilt, an empty cola bottle, cigarette stubs. Someone had clearly been sleeping there, having ended up homeless for some unknown reason. Ayami and Wolfi also had a Burger King meal. The square was full of people hurrying to catch a train, and those who had just come off a train, and/or were heading for the subway. A grand piano had been placed in front of the station colonnade. A shabbily dressed middle-aged man sat down at the piano and began to play. The intensity of his movements attracted the notice of passers-by. Those who had stopped to watch him were bumped into by those still walking, but it was the watchers, not the walkers, who eventually gave up and pressed on, while the walkers became watchers in turn. In front of the piano was an open briefcase containing notes and coins tossed in by appreciative listeners. Thick droplets of sweat collected on the pianist's jaw and plopped down onto the keyboard. A bird with a curved beak, grey back and yellow webbed feet alighted on the piano's wing-shaped lid. It flew off again after depositing some pale grey shit.

Wolfi chewed his hamburger hungrily.

'Back home I eat sushi from a paper lunch box,' he grumbled. 'Now I've come all the way to the Far East and end up with a Burger King. But I'll take it over hot rice.'

Pinching French fries between her fingers, Ayami thought Wolfi's voice made it sound as if he were complaining, even when he was just making conversation.

'Is it Schubert?' Wolfi muttered. 'It's too far away to hear properly. And the traffic's too loud.'

'It's jazz,' Ayami said. 'The melody's familiar, but the title isn't coming to me . . . and you're right it's too noisy to make it out properly. The noise of the traffic is like the sound when a field of barley is set on fire.'

'Huh? The sound of a barley field on fire? I've never heard that expression. I don't know what a barley field on fire sounds like. Were you born in the countryside?'

'Probably not. But I'm not sure.'

'What kind of answer is that?'

'I don't really remember. I left home when I was young.'

'But you'd still know, from your parents.'

'I was adopted.'

'Ah, I see.'

Just then, Ayami's phone rang. She cupped the receiver with her hand while she took the call, to block out the noise from their surroundings.

'Of course I'll listen to you,' Ayami said into the receiver. 'And you listen to me, too, please. Isn't that why you called?' She paused to listen, then spoke again. 'Yes, we'll discover an unknown place . . . like we always do. But not right now. Right now Yeoni is absent. Later, when she returns, she will become your cave. The third cave that exists simultaneously . . .'

'Were you talking to Yeoni just then?' Wolfi asked as soon as Ayami hung up. 'I didn't mean to eavesdrop, but I thought I heard the name "Yeoni". Though of course I might have misheard.'

'That's right, you misheard. "Yeoni" is a very common phoneme in Korean.'

'Ah, is that so?' Wolfi nodded, and they went back to eating in silence.

After a while Ayami's phone rang again.

'Of course I'll listen to you. And you listen to me, too, please. Isn't that why you called? . . . Yes, we'll discover an unknown place . . . like we always do. But not right now. Right now Yeoni is absent. Later, when she returns, she will become your cave. The third cave that exists simultaneously . . .'

'I'm awfully sorry, but . . .' Wolfi began again as soon as Ayami got off the phone, unable to suppress his curiosity. 'If you weren't talking to Yeoni, I'd be very grateful if you'd say, just briefly, what you were talking about. Because, though yours is a strange, foreign language I've never heard before, still I could tell that the two conversations were very similar. And then, the tone of your voice as you were speaking . . . it was very, well, particular. A particular voice talking about a particular moment in life, that was it. It makes me want to know what could be said in such a voice. All of a sudden, I'm curious about the acoustics of Korean. It sounded exceptionally secretive, distinct from the kind of standardised babble that fills the streets of the world's other big cities. Though I have no way of knowing whether that impression was produced by your voice, or because it was an especially private conversation. Of course, if it was private then naturally you don't have to tell me what it was. I'm asking purely out of musicological curiosity.'

'It's not private. I was recording a message for my answerphone. I was worried the first one might have got deleted by mistake, so I recorded it again to be sure.'

'Ah, I see.' Wolfi nodded. 'Strangely, when I heard you speak just then, the thought passed through my mind that "Yeoni" might be a Korean word for "secret".'

'It's just a phoneme, like I said. It doesn't mean anything in itself.'

Wolfi changed the subject, tilting his head upwards to look at something. 'When you told me earlier I couldn't quite picture it, but now I can see that you really are an actor. Your image is projected on that big screen up there. Is it a TV show? Some kind of performance film? A soap opera you used to be in?'

Just as he had said, a TV programme was being shown on the huge screen in the station plaza, with Ayami's face filling it entirely. This on-screen Ayami looked somewhat flustered, and her eyes shone as though filled with tears.

But she was not crying.

A studio resembling a theatre, complete with a stage. The host and Ayami sit in the centre. To the right of the studio is a door, and on a sofa, set back and a little to the left of Ayami, several people sit in a casual, relaxed-looking group. Each person is holding a cup of tea, and one is smoking a cigarette. In the middle of the back wall is a screen.

Host: Ladies and gentleman, this is *Family Reunion*. This week, live from our studio, we will witness the moving scene of a woman who lost her memory after parting from her family aged five, now finally reunited with her mother. We've compared their DNA, and the relationship is beyond doubt. Even if the woman still can't remember her own family, her parents say they never forgot her. So stay tuned and don't miss a single moving moment!

The door in the right-hand wall of the studio opens, and through it comes a middle-aged woman, hesitant in front of the camera, her long hair dyed an unnaturally deep black. The short woman's scrawny calves corded with stringy muscle, her pathetically small feet, her shoes that gleam like new yet look like cast-offs, are exposed in vivid detail by the camera. She looks almost as if she were done up for a play. The camera zooms in on what is visible of her face beneath a wide-brimmed hat. Framed by her long, excessively black hair, her tanned skin bears conspicuous pockmarks. Puckering her lips, the woman bursts into tears.

Woman in Hat (grasping Ayami's arm): Child! Yeoni!

(Ayami stands stiff and wordless. Her expression and body language are those of someone at a loss, unsure of how they should act.)

Woman in Hat (sobbing): Yeoni! Your mother is sorry!

Ayami (snatching her arm away): I'm not Yeoni.

Woman in Hat: Right, I know, I know . . . the TV people explained it to me. Your adoptive parents called you Ayami . . . but your real name is Yeoni.

Ayami (as though against her will): Yes, I heard that.

Host: It must be hard for both of you, I know. Still, this moving scene will remain with us for a long time. Miss Ayami, or Miss Yeoni, please sit down here, and let's go through everything slowly.

(Both Ayami and Woman in Hat sit on the sofa as instructed, next to the other panellists, who have been preparing questions while drinking their tea.)

Panellist 1: My sincere congratulations. How many years has it been, exactly, since you last saw each other?

Host: Let's see . . . it would be twenty-four years.

Panellist 1: I've been told that, in those twenty-four years, the mother tried so hard to find her daughter.

Woman in Hat: Yes, that's right. For several years after I lost her, I could hardly eat, I went up and down the country looking for her. Even now, when I think of it . . . (chokes up).

Panellist 2: After entrusting your child to relatives, you must have been very surprised to learn that their domestic situation was bad enough to make her run away.

Woman in Hat: Yes. At the time we were extremely poor . . . . And had many children.

Panellist 2: In those days, everyone was much poorer than they are now.

Panellist 1 (nodding): That's right, there were far more poor people then than are now . . . of course, far more children, too . . .

Woman in Hat: It wasn't just that – the child's father had an accident and ended up in hospital, so when my relative asked to take in our Yeoni, I thought it would be the best thing for the child. Of course I did – he was a civil servant, this relative, and high up too! We weren't sending her away to strangers, after all, so we could stay in touch now and then; we didn't see any reason for it not to work out. But my goodness, the child just up and vanished. Left the house without a word! A five-year-old! No one told us till several months later. Oh, I cried and cried. But, Yeoni, how tall you are! Your adoptive parents must have raised you well. Your brother and sisters are all quite short, like your father and I. You were too, when you were a child.

Panellist 2: Your relative was a high-grade civil servant . . .?

Woman in Hat: Yes, that's right. The mayor of Seoul, actually. Of course, this is a very distant relative. A cousin three times removed, at least. But family is family. We thought it would be much better for her to be with them than with strangers.

Host: I've been told that your family have come here with you today?

Woman in Hat: Yes, they're all here. Not the child's father, he died a long time ago, but she has six older sisters and an older brother.

Panellist 3: And you went and searched every orphanage in the country?

Woman in Hat: You don't know the half of it. It's because of our Yeoni that we started selling fruit in the first place – something we could do while we moved around. At each village we'd make sure to get a good look at any kids who were around the right age. At one time there was a rumour that our village pharmacist had taken a child with him when he disappeared . . . but, we never did find any leads, not even when we got the police involved, so eventually we assumed she had ended up in an orphanage, then been adopted and taken overseas.

Panellist 3: But you couldn't find her because her name had changed.

Woman in Hat: Yes, that's right. I would never have dreamed that she wouldn't be able to remember anything of her childhood. That she would even forget her own name. Child, Yeoni, your mother has lived her whole life regretting sending you away . . .

Ayami (as ever, with her expression and body language those of someone at a loss, unsure how they should act): I'm not Yeoni.

Host: OK, Miss Ayami. But since your original name was Yeoni, now you have two names. Let's hear your story, Miss Ayami. You were an actress?

Ayami: Yes, a stage actress.

Host: But we also have a film you appeared in. A performance film that was shown at a festival. Let's take a quick look.

On the screen to the rear of the studio, the interior of a Burger King appears. Ayami wears a starched white cotton hanbok, with no detailing or decoration. Her thick black hair is secured in a low ponytail, and rough hemp sandals poke out from beneath the hem of her skirt. Staring straight into the camera, Ayami speaks her lines in a harshly clipped voice.

I will – recite – a poem – so – give me – just one – coin.

A male actor jumps out from behind Ayami, phone in hand, and immediately starts gabbling: Be quiet, I just got a call from Greece, it's a secret so no one must listen in, but what's that? Oh dear, there's a nappy on the floor.

The screen returns to black.

Host: Had you been looking for your birth parents?

Ayami: No, actually . . . my adoptive parents told me that my birth parents had died, that there were no close relatives, so I hadn't tried to look for anyone.

Panellist 1: Where did your adoptive parents hear such a thing?

Ayami: From the orphanage.

Panellist 2: They must have been so surprised and happy to hear that it wasn't true, that your birth mother is still living.

Ayami: Well, no, because they're no longer with us. They both died the year I entered university.

Panellist 3: So young?

Ayami: Actually they were very old. When they adopted me they were already over sixty.

Panellist 1: What were they like?

Ayami: They were very affectionate, very friendly. They always treated me warmly. So it was hard for me when they suddenly passed away.

Panellist 2: You seem to have had a happy childhood – that will be some comfort to your family. It's lucky. What did your adoptive parents do?

Ayami: They . . . they were dog breeders. They had a place on the outskirts of Seoul. It closed, there's nothing left of it now, but I still go back now and then, whenever I think of them.

Panellist 3: So, Miss Ayami, your family situation now . . .

Host: Are you married?

Ayami: After my adoptive parents passed away I dropped out of university and got married. My husband was a salesman for a pharmaceutical company. But, unfortunately, some time ago, there was a bus accident . . .

Host: Are you saying he was killed?

Ayami (calmly): Yes.

Sighs of sympathy come from the audience off camera.

Host: In that case, Miss Ayami, you must be especially happy to be reunited now with your mother. After all this time with not a single person in this world you could call family . . . you must have been very lonely.

Woman in Hat: Yeoni, there's no need to worry about anything any more. You have me, and you have your sisters, and your brother. You even have nephews and nieces! The eldest is already married.

Host: Miss Ayami, is there anything you've been wanting to say to your mother? Or to ask her? Anything you're curious about? Please, don't hold back.

Ayami (hesitantly, towards Woman in Hat): Well . . . who gave me the name Yeoni?

Woman in Hat (a little flustered): That? Ah, that . . . actually, your father and I named your sisters and your brother but . . . you happened to be named by the pharmacist. The one who went missing. And so some bad people started the rumour that he had taken you away.

Ayami: You mean the pharmacist who was killed by a nail driven into the crown of his head?

Woman in Hat: No . . . that . . . well, it's such a horrible thing. But that was just a rumour; you were a child at the time so you wouldn't have known. (Shuddering) It makes the hairs on my arms stand up. How can you remember? It seems that's the only thing you haven't forgotten.

Ayami (in an especially clear voice): That's right, I haven't forgotten.

Host (sensing the tension, and trying to defuse it): It's a lot to take in, isn't it, Miss Ayami? An experience like this would be enough to leave anyone bewildered. You should be happy, true, but happiness itself is so unfamiliar to you. This must all be very difficult but, even so, could you tell us how you're feeling at this point?

Ayami: I'm not sure yet. I'm just bewildered.

Panellist 3: You were never curious about your birth parents?

Ayami: I was told . . . that they were just poor people.

Host: In those days everyone was poorer, right? There was much more poverty then.

Ayami: And later I heard that my birth father's distant relative had been the mayor of Seoul.

Panellist 1: You did? How would your adoptive parents have known that? But— wouldn't that have made it possible for you to find your birth parents?

Ayami: He was only a very distant relative, and I didn't know which mayor; besides, I'd been told my birth parents had died. There didn't seem much point. I didn't know I had sisters and a brother.

Host: Right! It's time to meet Miss Ayami's siblings, who've been waiting here in the studio. Miss Ayami, you must have long grown used to the idea of being alone in this world. Now, all of a sudden, you learn that you're the youngest of eight! Your heart must be racing, yes?

Ayami (still at a loss for how to behave): I'm not sure yet. I'm just bewildered.

Host (into the camera): Viewers, the waves of emotion will continue after a short break. Eight siblings are finally gathered together in the same place – and with their sons and daughters, too. What a big family! What a reunion! Don't switch over!

Using both index fingers, Wolfi was typing out the sentences that were coming into his head in a long rambling stream:

. . . Woke within a feeling of loneliness clogging his throat like smoke.

He found himself in a cramped, sweltering room.

A young woman sitting on the edge of the bed looked down at him. Her black hair hung over her white, sweat-damp forehead; her face was smooth and round as the moon.

'Where am I?' W asked.

'This is Seoul,' said the Moon woman with the shining forehead.

'Why did you wake me?' he asked, and the woman held out a phone.

'A call from your wife.'

He took the phone and spoke into it: 'I'm in Seoul; I seem to have been kidnapped by some woman. Do you know what country Seoul is in?'

'You don't have to make up any bullshit to prove you're a son of a bitch. Everyone knows that already. That's all I called to say.'

His wife slammed down the receiver, ending their conversation.

'It's insanely hot. If I don't have a cold shower I'll suffocate. I need to piss, too. My bladder's about to burst. Where's the bathroom?' W asked, handing the phone back to the woman.

'There isn't one. You can use the kitchen tap to wash yourself.'

'What?'

'The toilet is next to the building's main entrance.'

'What?'

'There's no need to act so shocked. Just imagine you're camping. I have to go out now, I have an appointment at the broadcasting studios.'

'Broadcasting studios? What are you talking about?'

'I'm appearing in a soap opera. Just a minor role. Today we're filming the scene where my family pressures me to marry an old man I don't like.'

'But . . .' W began hesitantly, 'it's not that important, but my editor told me you were forty-nine-years old, and that you're a German-language teacher.'

'Yes, I'm forty-nine. But I'm an actor, not a German teacher.'

'You really don't look forty-nine. Not that I've ever successfully guessed a woman's age.'

'I use expensive make-up. Even your mother would look this way if she used the same stuff.'

'Really?'

'It doesn't only make you look younger, it conceals any scars and imperfections. My face is actually covered with smallpox marks.'

'What?'

'Also, a while ago my ex-husband came to my workplace and slashed my face with a knife. I had to have twenty stitches. He was wildly jealous.'

'What?'

'There's no need for you to be afraid. He was crushed to death by a bus last night.'

'What? No, who are you?'

'I'm Yeoni from the northern desert.'

★

Ayami took out the poetry collection she'd been given at the exhibition, flipped through a few pages half-heartedly, then turned to Wolfi. 'How about we go out and find a cafe? It'll be easier for you to write somewhere with airconditioning. And it's too dark here. I thought writers usually worked in cafes and libraries.'

'I have to record whatever comes into my head in the same place it happens. Things occur to me as images, as forms, not as words arranged into sentences. The images quickly dissipate after the moment's passed, and once that happens there's no way for me to capture them in language. Recording them like this – I'm only making sketches, rough outlines. It doesn't matter where I am. Even when I'm not writing, I've always detested libraries and cafes.'

'Your hair's soaked with sweat.'

'So's yours. I mean, so is everyone's here.'

'What do you want to do, then?'

'Let's take a train. Since we happen to be at the station.'

'Where to?'

'Well . . . this is my first time in the Far East, but I've often wanted to go to the Yalu River.'

'Do you know where that is?'

'Not exactly. But I know it's on the border between Korea and China.'

'It's impossible.'

'What?'

'It's impossible to go there by train.'

'Why?'

'Because this country is more like an island than a peninsula; we're surrounded by the sea on three sides and the northern border can't be crossed just whenever someone feels like it; this isn't the European Union.'

'Ah, really? An island like Japan, then.'

'Yes. The country over the border is North Korea, you know.'

'Ah, yes. I'd completely forgotten. I guess we'll have to give up on the Yalu River.'

'So where do you want to go?'

'I just got the urge to get on a train, that's all.'

'So . . . . where?'

'Wherever the next train takes us.'

'What'll we do when we arrive?'

'That's not important. We'll take whichever train travels furthest, and stay on it through the night.'

'An express train would take us across the whole country in two hours. And reach the sea. There's nowhere further we could go. I told you, this place is like an island.'

'They can't all be fast trains. Slow ones exist, too. Night trains that go slowly on purpose, to arrive in the morning rather than the middle of the night.'

'I'll check the timetable.'

Ayami went into the station and, after a while, re-emerged.

'There's a night train going to Busan that leaves at 10.30 tonight and arrives early tomorrow morning. A Mugunghwa train. I bought tickets.'

'What's Mugunghwa?'

'The slowest class of train.'

'Ah.'

'It's a night train, but there aren't any beds. Mugunghwa is the cheapest train, as well as the slowest.'

'That doesn't matter. I won't sleep anyway.'

'In that case, let's go.'

'But, has the film finished? The performance film you're in.'

'It'll continue after the ads; I don't particularly want to watch it.'

'If only there were English subtitles,' Wolfi said regretfully. 'It seemed more like theatre than a film. Even what you called the Burger King scene. Though it was much shorter than I expected. Could you explain for me what exactly is going on?'

'It's an everyday story, of things that happen in a big family.'

'You mean, like the marriage of a daughter approaching marriageable age?'

'Right.'

'Ah, I see.' Wolfi nodded. 'I saw a Chinese film once with that kind of story.'

They walked side by side into the station, where once again Ayami's face was projected on a large TV screen. The second part of *Family Reunion* had started. But Ayami dragged Wolfi with her into a bakery for coffee, and told him they also had to buy some water from a shop.

'We want platform two,' Ayami said. 'If I don't get a coffee right now I might pass out. My vision's going blurry.'

'Didn't you say the train leaves at 10.30?' Wolfi grumbled. 'Why the rush? It's barely ten now.'

'The trains don't necessarily leave on time. They can leave much earlier than it says on the timetable. It's best to go to the platform early and wait.'

'Trains leave early? I find that hard to believe.'

The platform was empty when they arrived. Ayami dropped down onto a bench and drank her coffee, which was now lukewarm. They sat side by side and sipped their drinks. A single insect flew about, gleaming white in the lights.

'Your female protagonist . . . does she end up dead?' Ayami asked abruptly, her gaze fixed in front of her, not looking at Wolfi.

'Probably,' Wolfi answered. 'But wasn't it difficult to understand what I said? With me talking so fast?'

'A little, but I could get the gist of it. Besides, you write detective novels, and those generally feature a murder.'

'Right.'

'So, who did it?'

'At first, suspicion falls on the wildly jealous ex-husband. The female protagonist earns money from telephone sex, you see . . .'

'But he's not the real culprit?'

'Right, the murderer . . . well, the murder is connected to an unsolved event from twenty years previously. A doppelgänger incident. Readers later realise that the female protagonist is the ghost of the woman who had been murdered many years ago.'

'So the murderer is the same one from twenty years earlier?'

'That's correct. And no longer of this world. This structure popped into my head when we went to the photography exhibition and I was looking at *Honeymoon I*. I still haven't plotted it out concretely. Whenever I write a book, I come up with several alternative versions. I write down as many as I can, read through them and choose the one I like best. The story I'm telling you now is the most recent version, which I've thought up since coming to Seoul.'

'I see.' Ayami thought for a moment then asked, 'What happens to the other versions?'

'Well.' Wolfi shrugged, looking unsure. 'They remain eternally unknown.'

'Your female protagonist – how does she die?'

'She goes missing. Because she has no family it's some time before anyone notices that she's gone. Her corpse is discovered by chance.'

'Where?'

'In the roof of her house.'

'So she was murdered?'

'We can presume so. No one knows for sure. So much time has passed since her death that even an autopsy would reveal almost nothing. Twenty years later "She Two" appears: the woman's second self. "She Two" leaves Seoul on the night train, on an impromptu journey with a man she doesn't know very well; there's an unexpected blackout, someone slips into the carriage while the lights are off, their features impossible to make out in the darkness, and stabs her. This happens when they cross the bridge over the Yalu, which forms the border with China. What do you think?'

'That it simply couldn't happen like that. I already told you, it's impossible to take a train from here to the Chinese border.'

'Ah, that's right.' Wolfi shook his head. 'I forgot.'

While Wolfi and Ayami were talking, the platform filled with people: a shockingly large crowd in a shockingly short space of time. Like sardines in a can, thought Wolfi. Their enormous bags and suitcases made them look as if they were setting off on a long journey. No one spoke. Even the children were silent. Beneath the strange lighting their faces looked almost grey-green. One group, standing stiffly together like a collection of variously sized candles, stared at Ayami in her conspicuously plain starched cotton hanbok.

A shrunken old man, wearing a coat so oversized he was almost swallowed up by it, appeared from among the crowd and passed in front of them, tapping a cane. Though he was both the oldest and the most unsightly person on the platform, he also seemed to be the most alive, purely because he was moving. His sweat-soaked hair was plastered to his forehead and gave off a nasty, sour smell. With his tired eyes behind gleaming spectacle lenses, he was like a rheumy old goat facing the butcher's axe. Those milky eyes were the oldest of all his body's constituent parts. Hesitating, as though they still did not believe in their own ability to perceive the world, those eyes blinked ceaselessly and irregularly. At each spasmodic movement, the eyeballs themselves aged yet more rapidly.

Passing in front of Ayami, the old man's lips twitched, his drooping eyelids trembled; they had melted like fetid cheese. As if he were saying goodbye to her.

As if he were saying: Of course, I'm just an obscure old poet. I could never have imagined that someone like me would end up outliving all of you.

'I could never have imagined there would be so many people taking the night train,' Wolfi said, looking shocked. 'It's as though war has broken out and everyone's hurried out of their homes to seek refuge.'

'Take me to another world,' Ayami mumbled, seeming almost to beg, her gaze fixed on the aged poet's retreating figure as he tottered away among the crowd. 'Take me where you're going now – to that other world.'

Ayami's eyes shone as though filled with tears. But she was not crying.

'What?' Wolfi asked doubtfully. 'What did you just say?'

'Take me to another world.'

'You're the one who said it's impossible to go to the Yalu.'

Ayami didn't respond. Instead, her hand brushed the back of Wolfi's, and her middle finger touched the inside of his wrist. A brief gentle pressure, as if taking his pulse. In that moment, Wolfi was struck with the thought that Ayami was inviting him along, in her own particular way.

4

Ayami and the director sat on a bench beneath the statue in the square and drank wine from paper cups whose wax coating had grown tacky in the heat. The wine was tart and bitter. There was rubbish scattered around the bench: packaging from a Burger King meal, a dirty quilt, an empty cola bottle, cigarette stubs. Someone had clearly been sleeping there, having ended up homeless for some unknown reason. There wasn't much time before Ayami needed to leave for the airport. The two of them drank in silence for a while.

'Just now . . .' Ayami spoke slowly. 'Just now, when we were standing in the middle of the square, I was startled to see the world vanish in front of my eyes. The glaringly lit shops in the arcade, you yourself in one of them, choosing the wine – all of it extinguished without even a bang or a crack. It seemed as though my eyes had disappeared rather than the objects themselves. I raised my hand unconsciously and groped through the air in front of me. But when I blinked, there were forms in the darkness. Forms that didn't actually exist . . . made up of the contours of the square, the arcade, the street and the statue. Forms without substance, like ghosts flying slowly, too late. Souls left behind on earth even after the death of matter.'

'Perhaps that kind of blackout is a symptom of ageing,' the director murmured, lost in his own thoughts. 'Just like declining memory. No, to be more exact, it would be a symptom of disintegration, of something gradually wearing thin.'

'What is it that's gradually wearing thin?'

'Well, if I had to put a name to it . . . the sleep of whomever is dreaming us?'

'Just then, when the shop lights went off, it occurred to me that I'm no more than an imaginary woman in your dream.'

'If that's the case, I don't want to wake up.'

'If the one who's dreaming me is not an unknowable god but you yourself. If the dream is the product of your imagination.'

'Let's drink to the fact that we're the products of each other's imagination.'

Each wordlessly drained their cups. The director spoke again.

'When I went into the shop, I saw two sales clerks sitting behind the counter, one young and one old; as I went up to them I realised they were actually asleep, though their eyes were half open. Beneath the strange lighting their faces looked close to grey-green, like the faces of dead police. They didn't wake up until I'd chosen the wine and took it over. I had to rap my knuckles on the counter. The younger one just barely raised her eyelids and mumbled something at me. She seemed to be talking in her sleep.'

They looked at each other and smiled.

The white bus appeared on the otherwise empty elevated highway, going even faster than it had been before.

Have they been to the hospital already? Ayami wondered.

Inside the brightly lit bus several women were sitting around a table, their backs straight, each of them reading a book. In a corner at the back, the part of the bus in darkness, a man wearing monk's robes sat with his eyes closed.

Opposite their bench a large screen was fixed onto the wall of the station. As it was deep into the night, and with the city intermittently losing power, the screen gleamed a blank black like an enormous lacquer tray. Yet at a certain moment it spasmed like a corpse receiving an electric shock. An image appeared. But before that came the sound of the radio.

Daytime – Temperature – Thirty – Degrees – Celsius – Absence – Of wind – Absence – Of cloud – Please – Phone – Yeoni – Thirty – Degrees – Absence – Of wind – Absence – Of cloud – Daytime – City – Mirage – Scheduled – To appear – Absence – Of wind – Absence – Of cloud – Absence – Of colour – in – The sky – Absence – Phone – Yeoni . . . Yeoni . . .

'It's the news,' the director muttered. 'The midnight weather report. The shipping forecast, for sailors.'

'Does the weather come before the news, or after?' Ayami asked.

They stared quietly at the screen. When it eventually crackled to life, it broadcast not the news but a late-night literary talk show. This time there was no sound, so they could not tell what the panellists were getting so worked up about. But as soon as he saw a certain face fill the screen, the director exclaimed: 'That's the poet I met this afternoon.' He pointed to the face on the screen with his free hand, the one that wasn't holding the cup full of wine. 'But his name isn't coming to me. Kim something.'

'Do you mean the poet Kim Cheol-sseok?'

'Yes, that's right, Kim Cheol-sseok.'

The poet looked extremely old. The screen was filled with his faded grey hair, his hunched back, the slackened skin of his throat, and his tired eyes behind gleaming spectacle lenses. Those milky opaque eyes were the oldest of his body's constituent parts. Hesitating, as though they still did not believe in their own ability to perceive the world, those eyes blinked ceaselessly and irregularly. At each spasmodic movement, the eyeballs themselves aged yet more rapidly. His shoulders were narrow and exhausted, and droplets of saliva dangled from the corners of his lips. Judging by the shapes being made by those lips, he seemed to be reciting or quoting from some poetry, either his own or somebody else's.

> Don't go far away, even for just one day, because
> Because . . . a day is long, and
> I will wait for you.

Ayami spoke aloud, following the poet's lips, her voice flowing out through his mouth.

Of course, I'm just an obscure old poet. I could never have dreamed that someone like me would end up outliving all of you.

The director turned to face Ayami. 'Even when I was a student I had to work,' he said quietly. 'My family were poor. When I was young, the fact that life involved suffering seemed entirely natural to me. So I didn't think suffering was especially hard. After all, I had no opportunity to learn about other ways of living. But when I came back after studying abroad and was unable to find a good job, when I had to take on temp work, each day was extremely hard. It was the most difficult period of my life. That was probably when I started to become estranged from my wife, so night or day I felt alone. Each cell of my skin ached with loneliness . . . I struggled to find a place to exist, in this world that seemed to be rejecting me. I spent the days teaching, getting paid by the hour, or looking for work; and the nights doing whatever I could to make money. The thing I remember most vividly from that time is my stint driving a bus. It wasn't an ordinary city bus, more like a coach, the kind hired for events or for a particular destination, and only ever at night.

'One day the bus was booked by a young man, who asked me to drive all night. He was accompanied by six older women. Old enough that it would have been more appropriate to refer to them as Mother or Grandmother than Older sister.

'"Where are we going?" I asked. He told me he just wanted to be driven in circles around the downtown area, all night, with the central station as the locus. Extremely fast. He explained it was a long-held family tradition, which they performed whenever one of them died. The man was wearing monk's robes, and I was wearing the uniform of the bus company. The uniform was regulation, complete with an absurdly large cap. I had to be careful not to let it slip down my forehead, else it would have obscured my field of vision.

'So I drove through the night. I suffered from insomnia then, plagued by too many thoughts, and was actually grateful to have that kind of work. "We have to go as fast as possible," the young monk ordered. It was the dead of night, so the roads were understandably quiet, but I can't recall encountering another vehicle the entire time. I still can't make sense of it. Isn't Seoul known for its hellish traffic? And another thing: the roads and buildings were all pitch-black, not a single light was on. It was like being in a blind mirror . . . like being in a blind dream.

'At one point I did think I'd glimpsed a tank painted black, as camouflage, but that was probably a hallucination. My insomnia had left me in a state of extreme exhaustion. Blood-coloured flares were being let off. I don't know why. Each time a flare exploded, dead birds splattered down from the sky. A sharp tension filled the empty night, its origin unknown.

'I drove through the night, circling the central station. When dawn approached, the scene spread out in front of my eyes was one of keen-edged purple light murdering a vague grey darkness: its aged parent. Watery blood began to collect on rooftops, their contours thrown into stark relief against the blood-coloured sky. Like the premonition of a hazardous peace. The young monk, who had sat in silence the whole night, suddenly shouted: "Stop!" The older sisters looked up from their books as one, like well-trained chickens; the headless white rooster tied to the roof of the bus began crowing in response. Don't ask me how a headless rooster can crow. I parked the bus in the station square. It was early morning, so there was no one around. Not that I'd seen even a trace of another human apart from my passengers that entire night. The young monk and his six older sisters got off the bus. They walked away in an unknown direction. In a line, like pilgrims. The monk went in front, behind him the youngest sister – though she looked almost old enough to be his mother – and the rest of them following in order of age, with the oldest sister at the rear, inching forwards, her back severely bent.

'With all my senses hazy from exhaustion, I watched them retreat. That's right, I was unable to tear my gaze from the retreating figures of those women and the monk. Even after they had disappeared in the distance, I couldn't think of looking in any other direction. Turning my head would probably have cost me more energy than I had to give. I was unable even to shift in my seat, as though my spirit had departed my body. For some unknown reason, all the energy had been sucked out of me. I was assaulted by feelings of vertigo, a migraine tore through me. The pain was so severe it seemed every cell in my body was losing consciousness.

'Just then, a man walked into the empty, early-morning square. Lightly dressed, his arms stuck fast to his sides, he strode along swinging both hands, which were empty.

'He walked towards the statue in the middle of the square until he was standing in its shadow, where he stopped and then began twisting his hands and feet slowly, in a gesture like a stage actor's; at first I was convinced he was sending me some kind of greeting. But in reality the man was an epileptic, who had come to catch the very first train of the day but who was now having a seizure. That day, sitting blankly in the driver's seat, I was the sole witness to the dawn square slowly filling with his low, contorted scream.'

'Did he die?' Ayami asked.

'Did who die?'

'The epileptic who had a seizure in the square.'

'Well. This is something I heard after the fact, at the police station – apparently the man had only a minor seizure that day, but a few days later he fell into the river and drowned.'

They sat without speaking for a while. Having finished his wine, the director whistled softly into the night. The melody, familiar to Ayami, was from a jazz song called 'Someone Has Thrown Away the Piano on the Beach'.

The soundless screen turned itself off. The goat poet's image vanished before their eyes. Now all that remained in the square was the statue of the general, standing with his arm half raised, pointing in an unknown direction.

'I have to get going.' Crumpling the paper cup and discarding it next to the bench, Ayami stood up. 'Even in a taxi it'll take me an hour to get to the airport.'

'At this time of day you'll be there in forty minutes. Do you really have to go? You haven't heard from Yeoni again, have you?' The director clutched Ayami's arm.

'She's in hospital. That's the only reason she hasn't been in touch. The poet's due to arrive, and I have to meet him. A promise is a promise.'

'Stay another thirty minutes.'

'I'm already in danger of running late. And I might not be able to get a taxi immediately.' Ayami looked up and scanned the deserted road by the square. 'Never mind a taxi, apart from the white bus that went by just now I haven't seen a single other vehicle. This really is a strange night.'

'Stay just fifteen minutes; no, just ten minutes more. For God's sake . . . my head hurts so badly I don't even think I can stand.' The director rested his head on Ayami's chest.

'But . . .'

'It's true, my head hurts all of a sudden, like that night long ago when the bus went around and around. Like a huge nail being hammered into the crown of my head, that's how merciless the pain is.' The director clung to Ayami's body, his face contorted like that of someone in genuine agony. 'My stomach's churning so badly I feel like I might vomit.'

'If you want to vomit, you can vomit on me,' Ayami whispered low into his ear. 'If that's easier.'

The director tried to avert his head, but only partially succeeded. He was sick for a long time, retching from his

· 151 ·

chest. White, burning hot vomit ran down Ayami's blouse and splattered onto the ground.

'Like you wrote in that letter,' the director said, 'take me to another world.'

Ayami cradled the director's head, resting it quietly on her lap. Even when he had finished vomiting, she gently stroked his bloodied crown, from where the nail's thick head protruded. Ayami stroked him like that for a long time, as though the repetitive gesture might conjure a shamanic power – the only way of keeping together, in the same place and time, two human beings in the process of disintegrating.

Translator's Note

Six years ago, when I chose to translate Bae Suah, I knew just enough of the UK–US translation landscape to know the pressure on translated texts to 'represent' their culture (as though this could ever be singular), and just enough of Bae's writing to know that she was dismissed and even castigated for her 'un-Koreanness'.

This is my fourth time translating a book by Bae, and the more time I spend on a particular author, the more I become aware of what's particular to them – themes, motifs, and individual words that recur across books (not that there isn't also development, though a feminist reading might value circularity over linear progress), accruing different connotations as they appear in different contexts.

This, too, describes translation, which repeats the book in another language. Repetition not without change, but as a refrain. It comes after, reiterates, but also modulates. For the resonance.

With Bae especially, recurrence happens within the same book. The semantic differences between Korean and English mean that not every instance can be carried over (some would just be distractingly awkward, though a certain degree of awkwardness – clashing registers, unusual phrasing, precision that can seem pedantic – is, luckily, another hallmark of Bae's style). Out of the various options, I choose the word that fits the most instances. But I also want to hint at the spectrum of resonance, so while *unknown* is the trail we follow here, the same word recurs once as *undisclosed*, and in the title itself as *untold*.

Korean doesn't always mark plurals, but it needed to be night and day, singular, because this is a book not of progression but recurrence and, perhaps more than anything else, of oppositions – though oppositions set up only to be dissolved into one another: male / female, material / abstract, familiar / foreign, and all their permutations. *Poet woman* rather than *female poet*, and always *German-language* teacher, because Bae uses repetition to expose and even poke fun at linguistic conventions, and the societal categorisation they otherwise support.

Bae's oppositions are emphatically not binaries. Her books are filled with repetition, mirroring, echoing, overlapping – of characters, especially women, of times and places. *Simultaneously* is another thread-word studding the text. Simultaneity is a paradox, except when it's not. Night and day are simultaneous at the scale of the planet.

Perhaps *parallel* is the better word. Like the 38th parallel, the line at which the Korean peninsula was divided between the Soviet and American occupation zones at the end of World War II.

Simultaneity of difference, even opposition. Like Bae's others, this book is simultaneously a detective novel and a surreal, poetic fever dream. Inhabited both by abstract, mysterious characters who blur and overlap with one another, and by fleshly bodies, wrinkling, festering, leaking menstrual blood. An 'other world' is both another plane of consciousness and the northern half of the peninsula. As for which is more 'real' – more known, more accessible – that depends on your belief systems, what you value, and on your passport. For South Koreans like Bae, who grew up when foreign travel was all but banned, anywhere abroad might as well have been another world. Even now, transnational mobility is easier for white men like Wolfi, or anyone with a wealthy aunt.

The Koreanness of this book might be its most significant detail, tucked away unobtrusively in the corner of the frame. Blackouts, curfews, camouflaged tanks – this was South Korea in the '70s and '80s, under de jure or de facto military rule. Hulking concrete highways, alleys festooned with tangled cables, low houses that snake up the shoulders of mountains, vehicle lights ribboning along the river at night – this is the Seoul I've walked through countless times, a little more lost to gentrification each time I return. Simultaneous existence of opposites-that-aren't, utterly severed and intimately entangled – this is the Korean peninsula. When is peace hazardous? When it's a war that never actually ended, and whose legacy of divided families and transnational adoptions still structures lives today.

Bae Suah is not 'un-Korean', but she is a decidedly 'nonnational' writer. For one, she is also well known as a translator, figures whose loyalty is often questioned. Bae translates from German, but frequently the texts she works from are themselves translations of non-German sources, by other distinctively nonnational writers, like Sadeq Hedayat, with whom she finds affinity. The Korean has a clue right at the beginning, where the ghostly lines Ayami hears are footnoted as Bae's own 'modification' of a published Korean translation of the Spanish source – a game of Telephone to which the English adds yet another stage. Bae's books often contain instances of translation, but there is no neat, non-porous division between translation and not. Translation is always happening, though we don't always notice it. What language do Wolfi and Ayami speak? The 'original' is already a translation. And the *idea* of translation pervades the whole. Bae's translationism doesn't so much import the foreign into the domestic as render such categories, like the identity of the individual nation states with which they are entangled, every bit as unstable as that of 'individual' characters (the 'individual' is as dubious a proposition as the 'original').

Shamanism has been practised on the Korean peninsula since prehistoric times, distinct from but interrelated with Siberian-Mongolian traditions. While it is the latter that features heavily in Bae's recent work – "according to Siberian shamanism", she explained, "ayami is the name for the spirit that enters the shaman's body and communicates matters of the other world to them" – cultures do not develop separately, in isolation, but through exchange, in relation. This, too, describes translation.

Bae's engagement with shamanism and nomadism reaches back to a kinship before borders calcified and were armed (epitomised by the strip between the Koreas, a portent of what all our borders are becoming). Yet it is not some prelapsarian dream of frictionless mobility. (Lofty rhetoric around translation too often valorises the circulation of elite cultural products as though this has any impact on global inequalities of human cross-border movement.) Airports and train stations are portals to another world, but they feature all the trappings of our contemporary one: immigration queues, demands for proof of identity, and huddled masses resembling wartime refugees.

Oh, let me go put on some hanbok, is a popular joke when the issue of 'Koreanness' comes up. That Ayami spends so much time in hanbok – but only for a performance. What is being performed for us, and how much is tongue-in-cheek? Just as Ayami struggles to tell if the director and Wolfi are joking, we might wonder: is the joke on the reader, and if so, which reader? Perhaps the one who opens a 'foreign' book only to be disappointed by the lack of obvious cultural markers. Like travelling all the way to the exotic Far East and being taken to a Burger King.

When is one book written by more than one person? When are two books both the same and different? Is translation a mind-bending paradox, a run-of-the-mill banality, or a joke that misses the mark? Perhaps all three – simultaneously.

Deborah Smith, Berlin, October 2019